Kicking Addictive Habits Once and for All

KICKING ADDICTIVE HABITS ONCE AND FOR ALL

A Relapse-Prevention Guide

by

DENNIS C. DALEY

Lexington Books

D.C. Heath and Company • Lexington, Massachusetts • Toronto

Library of Congress Cataloging-in-Publication Data
Daley, Dennis C.

Kicking addictive habits once and for all: a relapse-prevention guide / Dennis C.
Daley.
p. cm.
ISBN 0-669-24329-9 (alk. paper)
ISBN 0-669-27879-3 (pbk.: alk. paper)
1. Compulsive behavior—Relapse—Prevention.   I. Title.
RC533.D34   1991
616.86'0651—dc20   90-20053
CIP

Published simultaneously in Canada
Printed in the United States of America
Casebound International Standard Book Number: 0-669-24329-9
Paperbound International Standard Book Number: 0-669-27879-3
Library of Congress Catalog Card Number: 90-20053

The paper used in this publication meets the minimum requirements of
American National Standard for Information Sciences—Permanence
of Paper for Printed Library Materials, ANSI Z39.48-1984.

∞™

Year and number of this printing:

94 8 7 6 5 4 3

To my wife Natalie and our two special children, Christopher and Lauren, who continue to bring much love and joy to my life, day in and day out. You guys are the greatest family a man could have.

Contents

Introduction

RELAPSE is the biggest concern for most people who get involved in recovery from any type of addictive disorder, whether it involves alcohol, drugs, food, gambling, sex, or some other behavior. Although there are differences between addictions, there are many similarities as well. The same holds true for relapse and relapse prevention. Causes of relapse are fairly similar across the various addictions. Alcoholics, drug addicts, compulsive overeaters, compulsive gamblers, and sex addicts all relapse in response to a common set of internal or external factors. There are many concepts of relapse prevention (RP) that I believe can be applied to different addictions.

RP has emerged during the past decade as a practical way for people to help themselves prevent a return to their addictive behavior, or to act quickly to cut off a relapse should one actually begin to occur. This book communicates many of the common-sense principles of RP. Information is provided on a broad range of RP topics. Many practical ideas are given on how to make changes in your thinking, behavior, and relationships. In addition, many self-awareness tasks are contained in this book that help the reader relate to the material in a very personal way.

The information in this book may be used as part of counseling or therapy, as part of a self-help program, or as part of a self-managed program of change. It was written for anyone interested in preventing relapse to an addiction or learning about RP. I think the reader will find my philosophy and approach very compatible with twelve-step recovery programs.

I have written many books and recovery guides, including several on relapse prevention for alcoholics and drug addicts.

As I travel about the country speaking on different problems, I am often asked for information on relapse prevention for addictions other than chemical dependencies. This book meets the need for information on RP that can be applied to any type of addiction.

This book is based on several different sources: my many years of counseling experience with individuals who have one or more addictions; my personal life experiences; studies and books written by professionals; books and guides written by people in recovery; and interviews and written surveys completed by anonymous members of various self-help programs. My interviews and survey were not conducted as part of a research study; instead, they were undertaken mainly to gather more material for the case studies. All of the case examples provided in this book were altered so that the identities of the individuals remain confidential.

Despite any limitations a reader may find in this book, my belief is that enough information and guidance are provided to help many individuals in their journey of recovery from an addiction. I have seen many addicted people make significant life changes and I hold much hope for the possibility of change.

Kicking
Addictive
Habits
Once and
for All

1

Understanding Addiction

Everybody liked Sarah. "I was a people pleaser," she said. "I never wanted to make waves or upset anyone. I was real overweight and very ashamed of how I looked. So I guess I tried to make up for it by being super nice to everyone. Problem is, I became a doormat and let people walk on me. Which only made me angrier. Which, in turn, gave me a great excuse to comfort myself with more food." Sarah weighed over two hundred pounds and ate compulsively. She often secretly binged in the car on the way to and from work. Sarah would even sometimes have "minibinges" in the middle of the night. She loved to cook and often prepared elaborate dinner parties. "The problem was, these were six- and seven-course meals, with only the best and richest of desserts. I actually ate modestly during these dinners. It was the leftovers that I could gorge myself on that I liked so much." Sarah also loved chocolate and all kinds of sweets. And junk food. Any kind of food actually. "I just loved to eat. I knew my love of food and excessive eating wasn't right, but I kept doing it. Eating became the most important thing in my life. I've been on every diet and weight-loss program there is. But I always seem to gain my weight back." Sadly, as her compulsive eating worsened, Sarah began staying at home more and avoiding her friends. She was very lonely and depressed. It never dawned on her that her compulsive overeating was the main source of her woes.

Frank drank a great deal of booze. "But," he said, "I don't even enjoy it anymore. It's just that I can't seem to stop myself. Even when I tell myself I'm only going to have a few drinks, it usually gets out of control. I'll be damned if I know why I do this. You think a grown man would know better." His father was also an alcoholic, but Frank swore he would never be like him or put his own family through what he had gone through while growing up. Frank once lost a job because of drinking. But he still drank. He had many blackouts and once even forgot how he had gotten home and where he had left his car. But he still drank. He was arrested twice for drunk driving and was once sent to DWI [driving while intoxicated] classes. But he still drank. His wife took their children and left him because she could no longer stand his drunkenness. But he still drank. His doctor finally convinced him to quit boozing. Frank took his advice and quit. In fact, Frank had quit many times. "I always go back. I just don't know why in the hell I let the booze take over and control me. Sometimes, I control it. I don't even drink every day, you know. Then my drinking gets out of hand again."

Debbie loved cocaine from the very first time she snorted it. "She was such a good kid and excellent student. Debbie was very popular at school," her mother said. "I don't know what went wrong. We gave her a good upbringing. Neither me or her dad used any drugs. And we hardly ever drank alcohol. Her brothers don't use drugs either." Debbie is a nurse who began experimenting with drugs while in high school and nursing school. During her last year of nursing school, Debbie discovered the magic of cocaine. "It was truly love at first snort. It felt so good, unlike anything I ever experienced. Sure, I knew about the dangers of cocaine, so I took it easy at first. But, when I graduated to freebasing, I really got out of control. When my addiction was at its worst, I stole pain pills and tranquilizers at work. Even sold drugs a couple times. All I know is that my addiction really screwed up my life and hurt my parents very deeply! God only knows what would've happened if I hadn't been forced to seek treatment." Fortunately for Debbie, she got caught stealing medications at work and was forced to get help or lose her nursing license. She now regularly submits urine samples and attends meetings for recovering nurses. Getting in trouble probably saved Debbie's nursing career and, quite possibly, her life.

John "collected" women. He was an avid reader of pornographic magazines and frequently viewed pornographic movies. John also masturbated compulsively. "My appetite for sex was very high. I felt I was leading a double life because I was a minister who was respected in the community, yet I was doing things that I publicly denounced and knew were wrong. This made me feel very shameful, which in turn led me back to sex, resulting in a vicious cycle. My job gave me plenty of opportunity to be with women. In many ways, I was a caring guy who wanted to help people. But, I couldn't separate sex from caring. I had no boundaries and gave in to every advance women made towards me. Usually, though, it was me who made the advance." John had even been arrested a couple times for exhibitionism years before. Once he was forced to go to a psychiatrist for treatment. "All I did then was substitute another sexual behavior for the exhibitionism, since I would've been in deep trouble if I got caught again. I was the perfect psychiatric patient . . . intelligent, willing to listen, and seemingly insightful. But this was all so superficial. My obsession with sex continued and I acted it out in a variety of ways. I just never told my doctor, so my addiction never got treated. I also ate too much and abused alcohol. I'm what I consider an addictive personality." John's addiction caused him quite a bit of suffering, upset his marriage, and affected his four children. They were virtually ignored for many years while he was busy with church work, which provided many opportunities to engage in compulsive sexual behaviors. It was only after many years, when John entered a self-help program for sex addicts combined with therapy with a psychologist, that he got hold of his addiction.

Bill was a sports fanatic who constantly bet on games. He was a compulsive gambler who was always watching games on television. In fact, it was not unusual for Bill to keep track of several games going on at the same time. Bill was an avid reader of sports magazines and the sports sections of several newspapers. "I sure know a lot about players, coaches, statistics, and all that stuff. It wasn't the game itself that I was really interested in," he said, "only the final score. I usually did pretty well and won more than I lost, although many times I took big losses. Like the last Super Bowl. Lost five grand. I was so furious that the Forty-Niners came from behind in the last few minutes to win the game that I shouted obscenities at the TV and even threw a glass at the TV, smashing the picture tube." Bill also frequently went to the race track, where he bet heavily. It was not unusual for him to drive more than three hours back and forth to the track after work. Of course, his wife and two sons seldom saw him. Oddly enough, his oldest son was a star athlete, but Bill managed to miss most of his games. His wife got very upset when she found out that Bill had taken out a second mortgage on their house without telling her. He had some heavy gambling debts to cover and his salary as a sales executive—which was very good—was not nearly enough. Bill had a feeling that he was going to "hit it big" one day and take care of his debts. Sadly, he did not see the serious nature of his addiction. In fact, Bill saw his problem simply as bad luck.

These stories show some of the more common types of addictions and how they affect the people who are addicted. Denial of the problem, guilt, shame, depression, self-hatred, confusion, and out-of-control behavior are just a few of the issues apparent in these stories. The experiences of these addicts also allude to the impact of their addictions on their families. Parents, spouses, children, and other relatives often are hurt deeply as a result of their involvement with an addicted family member. Seldom does an addicted person not affect several others, most often family members closely involved in his or her life.

We live in a society that both promotes and condones excessive and addictive behaviors. "More is better," "instant gratification," and "seek your pleasure" are the kinds of messages that bombard us constantly. Indeed, all of us probably have some behavior in which we engage excessively. But when excessive behavior is part of an addiction, we are facing a much more serious problem that is often very damaging to us and to others. Millions of people are addicted to one thing or another, and many have multiple addictions that wreak havoc with their lives.

Types and Prevalence of Addiction

Any substance that we ingest, or any activity or behavior that we engage in, can become an addictive habit or disorder. Addiction refers to a relationship with a substance or activity that is excessive or compulsive, causes problems in one or more areas of our lives, causes distress when we are not engaging in it, and often exerts a good deal of control over our lives, even when we are not engaging in the addictive behaviors. Addiction is better seen as a "disorder" with a characteristic set of symptoms rather than something that is easily or simplistically defined. In a later section, the symptoms associated with addiction will be discussed in more detail.

The more common substance-related addictions involve abuse of alcohol, tobacco, or other drugs; compulsive overeating; and compulsive dieting. The most commonly seen addictions related to activities or behaviors include compulsive sex, compulsive gambling, workaholism, making money and accumulating wealth, spending money, seeking power, and stealing or committing crimes. Even watching television and religion have been discussed in the context of addiction by some writers. Recently, attention has also been given to love and relationship addiction, as well as to the so-called positive addictions such as exercising, running, and meditation.

The personal pain—whether it is physical, emotional, or spiritual suffering—that goes along with any type of addiction is hard to quantify. Such pain certainly does not stand out when one looks at statistics. Nonetheless, let us look at some statistics for several of the addictions, keeping in mind that numbers in no way tell us anything about the specific people represented in these numbers.

- A recent report to the U.S. Congress entitled *Alcohol and Health* estimates that 18 million adults eighteen years of age and older currently are having problems as a result of alcohol use. Many of these people are addicted to alcohol.
- A major survey of over twenty thousand adults in the United States conducted by the National Institute of Mental Health reported that 13.7 percent of adults have experienced problems with alcohol use. About two-thirds of these were considered to have alcohol dependence. Almost half of the alcoholics in this survey had at least one additional problem, such as drug abuse or addiction, or a psychiatric illness.
- The same survey also reported that 5.9 percent of the adults studied had a problem with drug abuse or drug addiction.

- The American Psychiatric Association (APA) estimates the prevalence of pathological gambling to be 2 to 3 percent of the adult population. This means that several million adults have serious gambling problems.

- Millions of people suffer from compulsive overeating, anorexia (that is, refusal to maintain a healthy body weight, distorted body image, and intense fear of gaining weight), and/or bulimia (i.e., recurrent episodes of binge eating followed by self-induced vomiting or excessive use of laxatives).

- In addition to alcohol and drug problems, millions of Americans have problems with compulsive eating, gambling, or sex.

- According to national surveys of households, high school seniors, and military personnel by the National Institute on Drug Abuse, "widespread drug abuse remains a serious public health concern."

What these numbers show is that millions of people have problematic relationships with alcohol, drugs, overeating, sex, and/or gambling. What these numbers do not show is the personal tragedy frequently associated with addiction: serious physical, mental, or spiritual health problems, loss of dignity, and loss of important relationships—to name just a few.

DEGREES OF ADDICTION

There are different degrees of addiction in terms of number and severity of symptoms and effects on one's life. Not everyone is alike in their addiction. Some people are much more addicted or experience more serious consequences than others. Addiction is like other illnesses. For example, individuals with cancer or heart disease have it to varying degrees. One person may function quite well with cancer, while another may be close to death. Or one heart disease victim may function without limitations, while another may be greatly restricted in what he is able to do. The following examples illustrate differences in the symptoms and the effects of use between two drug addicts, one addicted to marijuana and the other addicted to heroin and cocaine.

Carol started using marijuana while a teenager. She occasionally gets high during the week, but parties heavily on the weekends, when she gets intoxicated several times. Her husband nags her to cut down and argues with her about her smoking. She sometimes coughs a lot after heavy weekend binges. Carol's motivation to finish a Master's degree has declined in recent years and she attributes this to her drug use. In fact, although she admits to being "hooked on pot," she doesn't think pot is a "heavy" drug that can cause serious problems in her life. After all, she says, she is well liked by her students and colleagues at the high school where she teaches, and she and her husband get along most of the time.

Catherine constantly obsesses about drugs and cannot get through the day without getting high. She will do anything to get drugs. Although Catherine will get high on just about anything, her preference is heroin and cocaine mixed together. She shoots these drugs into her veins with needles and hangs out mainly with other addicts. Her appearance has become ragged and she has lost over twenty pounds from not eating. Catherine was hospitalized twice following accidental drug overdoses and once for hepatitis resulting from using an unsterilized needle that she shared with another addict. Catherine relies on stealing and prostituting to get money for drugs, as she was fired from her last three jobs. She once got herpes from one of her clients after becoming careless and not using condoms. Her mother took legal custody of her two young children because Catherine was unable to provide proper care for them. Her day-to-day existence revolves around scheming to get drugs, getting them, and using them.

Figure 1–1, which relates specifically to alcohol and other drug use, shows a continuum of use and the related consequences. This same concept of a continuum can be applied to other addictive behaviors as well.

SIMILARITIES AMONG ADDICTIONS

Addictive diseases or habits, whether to substances such as cocaine or behaviors such as gambling, have some things in com-

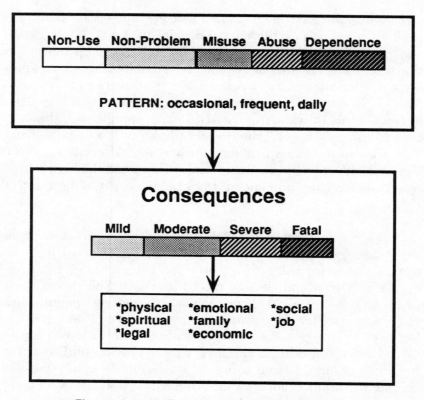

Figure 1–1. A Continuum of Substance Use

mon. They involve some form of indulgence that produces immediate pleasure or gratification. They also involve significant physical, emotional, or spiritual health risks. The costs are quite enormous in terms of personal suffering, costs to the public, and effects on the family.

Negative consequences, especially the more serious ones, such as medical problems that result from repeated involvement with an addiction, may not be experienced for a long time, sometimes after many years. For example, adverse health consequences associated with obesity or repeated vomiting (related to compulsive overeating) may not show for years. Gastritis, liver disease, and other organ damage caused by alcoholism may not be evident for years. Even when the individual intellectually knows the addiction is harmful or potentially harmful, the addictive substance use or behavior continues.

MULTIPLE ADDICTIONS

Many people are afflicted with two or more addictions. For example, it is not unusual for compulsive gamblers, compulsive overeaters, or sex addicts to have an alcohol or drug addiction. And it is very common for alcoholics to have a drug addiction. The previously mentioned community survey of twenty thousand adults in the United States showed that the rates of drug abuse and drug addiction were 270 percent higher among alcoholic men, and 620 percent higher among alcoholic women compared to the nonalcoholics in this survey. A study of patients in a treatment facility for chemical dependency found that almost one patient in five had a gambling-related problem. Of the patients studied, 9 percent met criteria for pathological gambling and an additional 10 percent showed signs of problematic gambling.

Sometimes the addictions are very closely related and feed each other. After John, the sex addict introduced at the beginning of this chapter, engaged in sexual behaviors, he felt anxious and shameful. He would frequently binge on food and wine in an attempt to make himself feel better. At other times, John would get high on wine before sexual acting out because it made him feel more comfortable and less guilty, at least for a short time.

Addictions are not always interrelated, however, and may develop or function independent of each other. Dennis, an alcoholic with an extremely serious gambling addiction, never drank when he gambled because it interfered with his concentration at poker games. When he stopped drinking and entered a recovery program, Dennis was unwilling at first to face his gambling addiction. He continued to gamble, yet did not drink. It was only after Dennis's wife left him because of his massive gambling debts that his therapist was able to convince him to deal with his gambling addiction.

Psychiatric Disorders and Addiction

There are many people with both an addictive disorder and another psychiatric illness, such as a depression, anxiety, or phobic disorder, to mention just a few. Rates of combined disorders are fairly high according to many different studies.

Dr. Roger Meyer, one of the leading experts on alcohol and drug addiction in the United States, has established that there are many possible relationships between chemical addictions and psychiatric illnesses. Following is a list and discussion of his ideas, which have been adapted to other addictions, not just alcoholism and drug addiction.

Having one type of disorder (an addiction or psychiatric illness) puts the individual at higher risk for developing the other type of disorder.

Psychiatric problems may modify the course of an addiction or the process of recovery from it.

Psychiatric problems may develop in the course of chronic involvement with an addictive substance or behavior.

Over time, the addiction and psychiatric symptoms often become linked together and interrelated, regardless of which one started first or which is more severe.

Sometimes these combined disorders are unrelated. One can develop long after the other or even when the individual is recovering from the first disorder.

Individuals with a psychiatric disorder are more at risk for addictions. Similarly, people with addictions are at risk for psychiatric disorders. The ECA survey, for example, found the following rates of psychiatric illnesses among alcoholics.

12.1 percent of the total population studied had a phobic disorder. The rate of phobic disorders was 1.5 to 2 times higher among the alcoholics.

1.5 percent of the total population studied had a panic disorder. Alcoholics were 2 to 3.5 times more likely to have this disorder than nonalcoholics.

6.6 percent of the total population studied had one of two different types of depressive illness. Alcoholics were 1.6 to 3 times more likely to have depression compared to non-alcoholics.

Less than 1 percent of the total population studied had mania, or bipolar disorder. Yet this serious mood disorder was found 3 to 10 times more often among alcoholics.

2.5 percent of the population studied had an antisocial personality disorder. Rates of this disorder among alcoholics was 4 to 12 times higher than among the nonalcoholics.

Psychiatric illness may affect how quickly an addiction develops. An individual with depression may, for example, turn to food binges, or alcohol or drug abuse in an attempt to feel better. In the process, an addiction may develop. Dr. Robert Cloninger's research on alcoholism has led him to classify different types of alcoholism. One type, which he labels "male-limited," develops in males at a young age, and is closely associated with antisocial behaviors. The men with this type of alcoholism are more prone to having a serious personality disorder in addition to addiction. Their addiction usually starts much earlier in life compared to the other type of alcoholics.

Psychiatric problems can also affect how addiction responds to treatment and often complicate recovery. Alcoholics and drug addicts with serious psychiatric disorders who get treatment for their addiction but not their psychiatric illness are at higher risk for relapse. Studies by Dr. Thomas McLelland and his colleagues of the University of Pennsylvania show that the rating of "psychiatric severity" is the single best predictor of relapse to alcohol or drug abuse. In other words, the people with combined disorders usually have the most difficult recovery.

Chronic involvement with an addictive substance or behavior may contribute to psychiatric symptoms. Sometimes, as in the cases of alcohol or drug addiction, this relates to the physiological effects of the substances. Many cocaine addicts report very serious depression when they "crash" from the effects of cocaine. This happens when they deplete the neurotransmitter dopamine in their brains. A reduction of dopamine is associated with depression. For many, suicidal thoughts or gestures come with serious depression. Users of PCP (angel dust), hallucinogens such as LSD, or uppers such as speed sometimes suffer psychotic breaks in which they lose contact with reality. They may develop paranoia (believing that others are talking about them or out to harm them), hallucinations (seeing or hearing things that do not exist in reality), or become delusional (developing unusual and irrational beliefs, such as that they are Jesus Christ or someone with special powers).

In other instances, the psychiatric symptoms are less related to the physical effects of a substance and more tied in to behaviors. For instance, depression may accompany a relapse to compulsive gambling, overeating, or sexual behavior. Or depression may occur when the addicted person realizes how much was lost due to the addiction. Health, relationships, status, self-esteem, money, and material possessions frequently are losses experienced by addicted individuals. Loss and depression sometimes go hand in hand.

Symptoms of addiction and psychiatric illness may become linked together over time. It becomes difficult if not impossible to separate them, as each affects the other. Often it is not even easy to tell which came first or which causes the most problems. Maggie, a compulsive overeater, berates herself badly following eating and purging binges. The messages she gives herself are: "I am a failure who is incapable of change. . . . I am a bad person. . . . I'm fat and unattractive. . . . I don't deserve anything but pain." Maggie then becomes quite depressed for weeks. In reality she's quite an attractive woman who has maintained a svelte figure by inducing vomiting after food binges. It was nothing for her to force herself to vomit a couple of times every day. Mike, an alcoholic with schizophrenia, drinks alcohol or takes street drugs to quell his anxiety when it rises very high or when the voices inside of his head become very strong. Although he medicates these symptoms, Mike becomes more reliant on alcohol and drugs. Since Mike is unable to consistently control his drinking, he often goes on binges once he starts drinking.

In some cases, addictive and psychiatric illnesses develop separately and are unrelated. Cheryl, a drug addict who had been clean for over two years, developed serious anxiety symptoms and panic attacks that greatly restricted her ability to function. Steve, a compulsive overeater who had lost eighty-three pounds and made significant improvements in his life during the previous year and a half, experienced serious mood disturbances. He would fall into deep depressions for several weeks and then switch into a manic or "high" state. When Steve's mood was elevated he did foolish things, such as purchasing expensive items he could not afford and did not need and going deeply into debt.

Characteristics of Addiction

Addictive disorders are multifaceted. Many factors contribute both to causing the addiction and to keeping it going. These include physiological, psychological, and social factors. The strength of these factors can vary with the addiction. Some addictions—such as those to alcohol, drugs, sex, and food—often involve a significant physiological component. Brain chemistry, metabolism, and physical processes within the body probably play a major role in these types of addictions. Some alcoholics and drug addicts, for example, believe they were "born addicted" and got hooked very early in life.

On the other hand, other addictive behaviors, such as gambling, may have less of a physiological basis and more of a psychological one. Expectations and beliefs, coping mechanisms, personality, and positive reinforcement (for example, financial rewards associated with gambling activities) are some psychological factors associated with addictive disorders.

Social factors may include the influences of an addict's family, peers, and ethnic group. The norms of important groups—school, church, community—can also play a role. Availability and opportunity are factors as well. Young people today are much more likely to use, abuse, and become addicted to drugs compared to youth in the 1960s. With the exception of alcohol, the most widely abused drug, all other types of drugs are more accessible and more widely used today than in previous generations. Another example of opportunity relates to gambling. States in which gambling is legal have higher rates of compulsive gambling problems. Certain types, such as casino gamblers, are attracted to live in areas that have legal gambling.

Regardless of the addiction, a generic formula that helps explain the causes is:

Body + thinking + emotions + personality + environment
+ coping skills + [alcohol, drugs, food, sex, gambling] =
ADDICTION

Why and how a person becomes addicted may not particularly matter at first. What is more important than finding the possible causes is to stop the addiction. Think of a burning building. Flames have engulfed it entirely. Firefighters are not going to try to figure out what caused the fire; instead, they will work to put it out. Later, when the fire has been extinguished, they will search for possible causes. The same is true for an addicted person. The fire of addiction first needs to be put out. Later, the person is in better shape to search for what may have caused the addiction.

Negative effects on various areas of functioning characterize addiction. Medical, family, job, relationship, financial, and spiritual problems are very commonly found among addicts. Addiction also tends to be progressive. It usually gets worse if not stopped and if the person never enters some type of recovery program. Certain types of addictions are potentially fatal. For example, premature deaths from accidents, suicides, and medical diseases occur with greater frequency among tobacco addicts, alcoholics, drug addicts, and compulsive overeaters than among people who do not have these addictions.

Now the good news! *Addictive illnesses are very treatable.* Hundreds of thousands of people have stopped their addictive habits and put their lives back together. Many have not only stopped the addiction but have developed into healthier, happier, and better people as a result of participation in recovery programs. Help from professionals and other recovering addicts in self-help programs such as Alcoholics Anonymous, Narcotics Anonymous, Overeaters Anonymous, Gamblers Anonymous, Smokers Anonymous, and Sexaholics Anonymous has enabled many people to enjoy the immense rewards offered by recovery.

THE SYMPTOMS OF ADDICTION

Although each particular addiction has its own specific signs, some common symptoms are associated with addictive habits or disorders. The number of these symptoms will vary among people. Some people will have every symptom; others will have just a few. The severity of the symptoms will vary, as will the consequences. The more common symptoms are listed in the following sections.

Excessiveness or compulsiveness. The substance or behavior is engaged in excessively (too much and/or too often); or the person feels a compelling desire for it. Fred, a sex addict, feels compelled to have sex several times a day. He states, "If I can't find willing partners, I'll go masturbate, even in my office or the men's room at work. Or, I might go out to a dirty book store and masturbate while watching movies in the booths." The addictive behavior is often irrational and makes little sense to an outsider, or even to the addicted person. The nature of addiction is such that logic alone cannot explain it.

Engaging in the addictive behavior for longer than intended or using more of the addictive substance than intended. Once the person engages in the addictive behavior, it is difficult to consistently control it. The self-help programs refer to this symptom as "powerlessness," which means that the individual has lost control of the use of the substance or the behavior. When Kathy, a gambling addict, goes to the track, she promises she will not lose more than fifty dollars. "Many times," she says, "I bet all the money I take with me. I always take more than fifty dollars just in case I need it. Sometimes I blow my entire paycheck, thinking I'm bound to hit it big if I keep betting." A compulsive overeater, Hal promises himself that he will make only one trip to the dinner buffets during vacations. But, he usually ends up going back several times. "I feel like I can't stop myself from going back for more," he says. "I go to the buffets every day and always get out of control on vacations. Where I eat becomes even more important than where I go for vacation."

Repeated attempts or desires to cut down or stop. The person may cut down significantly, or even stop the addictive behavior completely, but only temporarily. The addicted person may stop many times, only to go back to the addiction. Or, the desire to stop or cut down may be present, but the person feels unable to do anything about it. Bruce, a gay man who is both a sex addict and an alcoholic, has experienced this symptom with both addictions. "Several times I stopped drinking completely for up to three months, but always went back to booze. There were many times in which I actually limited myself to only two or three cocktails per occasion. But I always ended up getting to the point where I had to get sloshed." In relation to his sexual addiction, Bruce says, "I go for awhile and have sex only with my partner. Then, I get these periods in which I pick up a lot of different men and sleep with them. And it's not like the seventies when you didn't have to worry about AIDS. It's dangerous and I sure don't know why in the hell I do it." This symptom is another example of powerlessness.

Denial. The hallmark symptom of addiction is denial: not seeing or not accepting the addiction and the need for recovery. This symptom shows in many ways and in such statements to oneself as, "I don't have a problem. . . . It's not that bad. . . . I don't always get out of control. . . . Well, maybe I have a problem, but I can control it if I try harder. . . . I'm not causing anybody any harm." Addictive disorders are often referred to as ones in which the main symptom is not knowing you have the disorder. Denial accounts for the fact that the overwhelming majority of people with an addiction never get help.

Obsession or preoccupation with the addictive substance or behavior. Too much mental energy or thought goes to the addiction or to the rituals associated with it. Al, a sex addict, says, "I constantly obsess about picking up partners, both men and women—where I can cruise, what I'll say, who I will try to pick up, what they will look like or be wearing. Or, I might spend hours figuring out how I can watch people undress or have sex. I've even hidden in the woods at a hangout where local teenagers go to neck, hoping to see some action." Diane spends quite a bit of energy on figuring out how to get drugs to feed her habit. "Or," she says, "I work on schemes to get money to buy my dope. I think I get off on the scheming as much as I do on the dope. This shit definitely controls my mind and behavior." Howard, a compulsive overeater, says, "I'm already thinking about lunch when eating breakfast. Or, thinking about dinner when eating lunch."

Changes in tolerance. This symptom, in which repeated use of the same dose has a diminished effect, typically is associated with chemical addictions. Or the addict may find that the amount of alcohol or drugs once used cannot be tolerated any longer, that the tolerance has gone down quite a bit and the high comes much more quickly with less of the substance. Other types of addicts also describe tolerance changes. Julie seldom is satisfied with what she calls "regular, or normal" sex. "I need more deviant or risky things to turn me on. So I might invite a couple men to have sex with me at the same time. I've even gotten into bondage, which was something I thought was real kinky and certainly something I would never do. Lately, I began to have sex in public places where there was a chance I could get caught. I've had sex with men in offices, classrooms in schools, and even in church, if you can believe that. The idea of getting away with sex in a public place was quite exciting. It was even more exciting if it was with a stranger." Julie's problem was that, as she engaged in more of these risqué behaviors, she became less satisfied with other kinds of sexual experiences.

Withdrawal. When the substance or activity is stopped completely, or even cut down, the individual experiences discomfort and some type of physiological and/or psychological distress. Although withdrawal is more commonly associated with alcohol or drug addictions, people with other types of addiction sometimes describe irritability, anxiety, depression, and strong craving for the addictive object when they stop their addictions. Interestingly, the basic recovery text of the Augustine Fellowship, entitled *Sex and Love Addicts Anonymous*, devotes an entire chapter to "The Withdrawal Experience." To many sex addicts, withdrawal is a powerful and painful experience.

Problems resulting from the use of an addictive substance or from an addictive behavior (unmanageability). An addictive relationship with any substance, activity, or behavior will result in some type of problem in one's life. Addicts report many problems related to family, work, income, law, society, relationships, and spiritual and physical health. Usually, but not always, the more severe the addiction, the more problems will accumulate. However, certain addictions, such as to the drug cocaine, can produce very serious problems in a relatively short time. If you refer back to the cases at the beginning of this chapter, you will see that not one of the five addicted people described was free of problems arising from addiction. In fact, if more details were provided about each of their lives, you would see more specific kinds of problems caused or worsened by their addiction.

Continuing the addiction despite its problems. This is one of the ways in which denial rears its ugly head. Many doctors, attorneys, family members, and friends have encouraged addicted people to stop their addictions and get help, only for the addicts to ignore their advice and continue. I have worked with alcoholics who continued drinking despite serious liver disease, sex addicts who continued deviant sexual behaviors despite being on probation and faced with jail if they were caught, and with gamblers who continued to gamble despite being threatened with the loss of their families.

THE CONSEQUENCES OF ADDICTION

Jack is a thirty-seven-year-old father of two children who has struggled with his weight ever since he was a young boy. He says, "I've been overweight my entire life. But it's been in the last ten years that my eating really got out of control. Although I was always heavy, I ballooned to almost three hundred pounds. I snuck food the same way an alcoholic sneaks alcohol. Bakeries were to me what bars are to some alcoholics. My health was shot. I had high blood pressure, quite a bit of GI distress, and was always seeing the doctor for one thing or another. In fact, I was a 'doctor shopper,' always looking for someone else to have the answer to my problems, rather than looking within at what I could do to help myself. Even little things like tying my shoes and walking up and down stairs became real chores for me because I could hardly bend over, and I tired so easily. My wife got turned off by my appearance. And you could forget about sex. I quit bothering her because it was difficult to perform, plus my weight made it hard on her. When I thought that she wanted sex, I'd pick a fight with her about some dumb little thing because I knew if she was mad at me, I wouldn't have to worry about sex. My kids were embarrassed by my appearance. And, although nobody knows this, I spent a good deal of money on food and snacks for myself. I'd lie to my wife, tell her I spent money on some tools or something for my workshop when I spent it on food. The worst part of all of this was I lost my self-respect and dignity. I felt pretty bad about myself. This probably played a big role in my bad moods and depressions."

The tragedy of addiction is seen in this brief case. Jack is not unique by any means. Not only did he experience the negative effects of addiction, but so did his family. Like Jack, people addicted to alcohol, tobacco, drugs, sex, gambling, food, and other things will usually suffer damage in one or more of the following areas:

Physical health

Mental or emotional health

Family relationships

Relationships with friends

Social and recreational activities

Spiritual health

Financial situation

School or work

Sexual addictions, compulsive gambling, alcoholism, and drug addiction often cause legal problems as well. These may result from breaking the law or getting involved in the judicial system through separations or divorces. Interestingly, the internal, personal pain experienced by addicts is often described as much worse than any physical discomfort, even serious withdrawal symptoms. As one addict so aptly put it, "Withdrawing from drugs ain't nothing like facing the shit addiction does to you and your family. That kind of pain is harder, 'cause you don't know when it'll go away. At least you know when drugs make you sick you'll feel okay in a couple days. When you don't care about nothing but getting fucked up and then get your shit together, then the real problems start. Believe me, getting sick was nothing compared to hearing my kids tell me how much they hated me for all the rotten shit I did during my addiction."

How to Tell If You Have an Addiction

The chances are that if you are reading this book you have one or more addictions. Unless of course, you are reading this out of general interest or for some other reason. There are several ways you can tell, however, if you are not sure where you stand. One is to review the symptoms of addiction on pages 15–18 and note those with which you identify. Another is to make a list of all the symptoms and behaviors presented in the different case histories in this book with which you identify. Do any of the stories seem to be addressing you? If so, which ones and in what ways?

Another way is to rigorously and honestly complete checklists of behaviors and/or symptoms associated with specific addictions. All of the self-help programs—to list only a few, Alcoholics Anonymous (AA), Narcotics Anonymous (NA), Overeaters Anonymous (OA), Gamblers Anonymous (GA), Sexaholics Anonymous (SA), Sex and Love Addicts Anonymous (SLAA)— have developed their own recovery literature, including pamphlets, books, tapes, and films. Most of these programs have what is referred to as a "big book" or "basic text," which is a book written by addicts for addicts that explains addiction and recovery, using the experiences of others in recovery. Each self-help program also has a pamphlet with a set of questions associated with the particular addiction that it addresses. Simply getting hold of these questionnaires and completing them can help you determine where you stand.

You can also read pamphlets and books written by professionals or recovering people. Or you can attend the meetings of self-help programs and listen to the stories of other recovering addicts, or participate in discussions on addiction and recovery. Seeing a professional therapist—psychiatrist, psychologist, social worker, counselor, and so on—can help as well. Make sure you choose one who understands addiction. Asking friends, recovering people in self-help programs, or your doctor for recommendations can help you find the right person. Calling agencies or professionals who advertise that they deal with addictive disorders is yet another possible road to take.

Some people keep a written journal over a period of time to keep track of the behavior they are concerned about. The journal can list the behavior engaged in (for example, alcohol use, binge eating, gambling, and so on), where and when it occurred, and what the consequences were. After keeping such a journal, an attorney was amazed at how much he drank. Since he tended to drink alcohol throughout the day, he never perceived himself as having trouble because he seldom felt drunk. However, his journal revealed a pattern of drinking seven to fifteen drinks per day, smoking a pack and a half of cigarettes each day, drinking massive amounts of caffeine in coffee and colas, and smoking four to seven marijuana cigarettes per week. His journal also revealed several missed and cancelled meetings resulting from extended lunches at the bar, and increased argumentativeness with his teenage son following a few drinks each evening after work. He also realized that his trouble sleeping and his feelings of depression and anxiety were worsened, or even perhaps caused, by his excessive daily drinking. When he recognized the extent of his substance use, he made a decision to cut down. After a few months of ups and downs and not being able to cut down very much, he finally decided that he was an alcoholic and had to stop completely. He became sober and has improved significantly since entering a recovery program.

Self-Assessment Questions

Following are some self-assessment questions aimed at helping you decide where you are in relation to an addiction. Answer these as honestly as you can. You may wish to discuss the results with a professional experienced in dealing with addiction, another addict who is active in a recovery program, or someone else you trust.

1. What are the substance(s) or behavior(s) that you are concerned about possibly being addicted to? When did you start these, and how long have you been involved with them? How much, and how often, do you use the substance(s) or participate in the behavior?

2. What is your usual pattern of engaging in this behavior (for example: every day, several times each week, several times per month), and how has it changed over the past several years (that is, is it getting worse)?

3. How has this substance or behavior affected your physical health?

4. How has this substance or behavior affected your thinking patterns, concentration, or attitudes?

5. How has this substance or behavior affected your moods or feelings?

6. How has this substance or addiction affected your behavior?

7. How has this substance or behavior affected your personality?

8. How has this substance or behavior affected your self-esteem?

9. How has this substance or behavior affected your motivation and your job or school performance?

10. How has this substance or behavior affected your financial condition?

11. How has this substance or behavior affected your relationships with your family, including your children?

12. How has this substance or behavior affected your relationships with friends or other people?

13. How has this substance or behavior affected your ability to conform to the laws of society?

14. How has this substance or behavior affected your religious beliefs and/or your spirituality?

15. What other ways has this substance or behavior affected you?

16. Who in your life has expressed concern over your possible addictive use of a substance or involvement in an addictive behavior? What exactly was the nature of this concern?

17. How would your life be different if you did not use this substance or engage in this behavior?

18. After reviewing your answers to these questions, what conclusions do you reach about yourself in terms of addiction(s)?

Only with rigorous honesty can you begin to face your addictions and start on the road to recovery. If you reach the conclusion that you have an addiction after reading this chapter, then I strongly urge you to join a self-help program and consider the possibility of seeing a professional therapist if you are not already doing so. Since not all addicted people need professional treatment, it is difficult to state in which cases it is needed. Any concerns you have regarding whether you need such help should be discussed with a professional.

2

Recovery from Addictive Disorders

Recovery as Abstinence and Change

"Diets just weren't enough." "I tried at least a dozen different diets over the years. Oh, some of them worked, . . . but only for a little while. My weight went up and down. So did my self-esteem. In fact, whenever I failed a diet I beat myself up pretty hard, and ended up depressed.

"Recently, I took another approach to my compulsive overeating. I finally realized that diet was only part of the solution. I had to change a whole bunch of stuff about myself and how I lived before my compulsive eating stopped and the weight stayed off. My attitude, my thinking about food, relationships, and myself, my behaviors, and how I got my needs satisfied were just some of the areas I changed as part of my recovery program.

"For one thing, I had to shop differently for food. No more free-for-alls in supermarkets, coming home with bags of high-calorie junk food (which I used to love). I went with a list of food to buy for only the next week. I cut way back on buying cookbooks and magazines. And, I made fewer trips to stores to buy cooking gadgets for my kitchen. All of this helped me change my attitude and take the focus off of food. I even consciously worked at not spending so much time sharing recipes with others or discussing food dishes I had eaten.

"Perhaps the biggest change was learning to get nurturance from my relationships with others, not from food. Even though I was friendly and talkative on the surface, I never let anyone really get close to me until recent years. I had to let others give to me rather than me always being the one to give to them. When I was real heavy I kinda felt I had to compensate by always trying to attend to the needs of others.

"Since I had been a master of stuffing my anger, I had to learn to let myself get mad at others and speak my mind. This was no easy task, but I'm no longer stuffing my feelings when I get ticked off." —Sylvia, age 42.

"I had to learn to separate love from sex." "My compulsive sexual behavior wreaked havoc with my life. I lost my family, my dignity, and sense of purpose in life. At one point, I became very depressed and even questioned if it were worth going on.

"But, for whatever reason, I hung in there. After I really surrendered to my sick compulsion, I made a serious commitment to change. I started by getting rid of my porno magazines and tapes. I busted my videos up with a hammer in my garage. It was like a symbolic release of my anger for being controlled by my strong sexual compulsions. I threw away my phone book with numbers of lovers and prostitutes.

"Some of my routines and habits changed. I stopped going out to bars and clubs because *every* time I drank, even just two drinks, my sexual compulsion reared its ugly head. For a while, I stopped going to the health club because of my tendency to hit on the women there. I bought a weight system and began working out at home instead. Later, when I felt able to go back to the health club, I took a friend along with me.

"Probably the biggest change was in my relationships and my views of love. Quite simply, I had to change how I related to people. This required me to look at my many character defects and to stop being so damn self-centered. God, this was as hard to change as everyone in SA [Sexaholics Anonymous] said it would be. I started with my family. Took a real interest in my parents and brother's family. Giving love to others felt wonderful. For a long time, I had been incapable of loving others.

"Outside of my family, this issue was more complex. I had to learn that sex and love were different. I used to fool myself in the past, operating under the illusion that if someone had sex with me, they were filling my needs for love. The truth is, sex was usually meaningless and empty because I hardly knew any of my partners at all. They were merely sex objects to me.

"Eventually, I got involved in a relationship with a woman that was not based solely on sex and meeting my selfish needs. I worked hard at becoming intimate with her emotionally. I learned to listen to her and take an interest in her ideas, opinions, and experiences. And, I learned to respond to her needs. Our relationship is give and take. I'm getting better and feel I've regained my dignity." —Greg, age 31.

As these two cases show, recovery goes beyond simply stopping an addictive behavior. It involves *changing*—attitudes, thinking, behaviors, lifestyle, and relationships.

Sylvia changed her attitudes about diets and food, and Greg changed his attitudes about love and sex. Sylvia changed her behaviors by shopping differently for food, spending much less time reading cookbooks and food-related magazines, and talking less about food and recipes with friends. Greg changed his behaviors by getting rid of his pornography collection and telephone book of sex partners, and by no longer going to bars or the health club to pick up sex partners. Both Sylvia and Greg changed their interpersonal relationships as well. Sylvia learned to get nurturance from others and stop stuffing her anger. Greg learned to give love to others and take an interest in his partner so that his relationship was not one-sided and focused on him and his needs.

Components of Recovery

Recovery from an addictive disorder refers to the process of stopping your addictive or compulsive behaviors, changing yourself, and changing your lifestyle. While many elements of recovery may relate to any type of addictive disorder, each addiction has some unique recovery issues. For example, a compulsive overeater often has to consider issues such as how to shop for food or eat in restaurants without going overboard. An alcoholic has to consider how to deal with events (weddings, office parties, and so on) where alcohol is served. A compulsive sex addict whose pattern of addiction includes daily masturbation has to examine how to deal with impulses to masturbate.

A number of key components of recovery are pertinent to all types of addictive disorders. These key components include:

your attitudes and motivations,

your beliefs and expectations,

learning information,

developing new coping skills, and

having a program for change.

Your *attitudes and motivations* toward recovery are very critical. Motivation may be external or internal. Obviously, the more you want recovery, the better things should go, as you will work harder at changing. However, in the early phases of recovery it is usual to not want recovery. Negative attitudes are very common. Many people embark on a recovery journey because they have to or are forced to by people (families, bosses, courts) or circumstances in their lives. Such motivation is external.

Your desire for recovery may change from day to day at first. Even if you stop your addictive behavior because of some external reason—such as saving a relationship, saving a job, or staying out of legal difficulties—you still can get well. Eventually, though, your desire to recover must become internalized. If you do not reach the point where you are recovering because *you* want it, you are more susceptible to relapse.

Steve, an alcoholic who went through a couple of different treatment programs before internalizing the desire for recovery, puts this in perspective. "The first time I went to treatment, it was to save my job. The second time I went, it was to save my marriage. Now, I did stay sober for a while. But it didn't last. The last time I went to treatment, it was for me! Because I wanted it." On the other hand, some people go to treatment for external reasons, yet internalize the desire for recovery quickly. Diana sought help for compulsive overeating. "I got help at first to keep my husband off my back," she said. "However, it didn't take me long to realize I wanted to deal with my compulsion to eat for me, not my husband. I knew I had to do it for myself."

Your *beliefs and expectations* about recovery are also very important. If you expect to do well in making personal and lifestyle changes, you are more likely to actually do well. Believing that you can deal with problems in your life or with the risk of relapse puts you in a better position to cope in a positive manner and not to relapse to your addictive behavior. On the other hand, if you expect to relapse or feel miserable, this is more likely to happen. If you believe recovery will be miserable and boring, then it probably will be. Your expectations and beliefs guide your behaviors and affect your satisfaction.

Al, a compulsive gambler, never managed to stay away from gambling for more than a few months at a time. "I didn't think I could do it. I wanted some action and believed I wasn't strong enough to resist making bets." Al's belief affected his decision to gamble. Nancy, another compulsive gambler, had a different experience. She said, "I expected recovery to be hard, but I prepared for it. I told myself I'd do whatever it takes to not gamble. It was that important that I not relapse, especially since I had put my family through so much, and I put myself through a lot, too. I believed I could weather temptations to gamble." Nancy's belief in her ability to handle temptations and problems and to not gamble was a crucial factor in preventing relapse.

Learning information is another key element of recovery. The more you learn about addiction and recovery, the better prepared you will be to handle the rough spots. Information can help reduce your anxieties, help you know what to expect during the various phases of recovery, and help you develop a solid recovery and relapse-prevention plan. Information often helps raise self-awareness and paves the way for making some of the specific changes you need to undertake.

Jim learned that it is normal to experience cravings for drugs, even after being clean for a few weeks. He also learned that cravings do not linger, and that they usually decrease in intensity and frequency as recovery progresses. This information helped him deal with his cravings. Knowing that cravings were normal and what to do with them allowed him to change his view of himself and what he could do to cope. Prior to learning this information, Jim had misinterpreted his drug cravings as a sign of weakness and poor motivation. His response, typically, had been to give in to his craving and get high.

Stopping an addictive disorder also requires *developing new coping skills.* New skills are needed to help you deal with thoughts, feelings, stresses, and problems that put you at risk for relapse. An addiction is one mechanism for dealing with feelings, problems, or stresses, even though it causes self-destruction in the process. Losing addiction as a coping mechanism means that you need to find new methods of coping. Learning such skills takes time and practice. You have to get used to applying them in your daily life.

Fred, a personable and handsome man, was recovering from a sexual addiction. He received many invitations from women to go out on dates. Since dates with women he did not know very well presented a high risk of relapse to him, Fred had to learn ways of refusing dates with these women. Later in his recovery, when Fred began dating again, he had to learn how to go out on a date without making it primarily a sexual encounter. His pattern had been to become sexual too quickly, often before he knew very much about the women he met. Keeping the conversation off of sex and going to places where he would not have privacy with his date were two strategies he initially used. He also learned to cope with his sexual desires by talking these over with a close male friend. This strategy allowed him an opportunity to get things off his chest and evaluate his options. Fred's new coping methods played an important role in preventing his sexual impulses from getting out of control.

The final component of recovery is a *program for change.* A program means a formal or informal plan of action to help you in your daily recovery. A program for change may involve psychotherapy with a professional, such as a psychiatrist, a psychologist, a social worker, or another type of therapist. It may also involve participating in self-help programs for your specific addiction or addictions. A program of change should include self-management activities. These are strategies or techniques that you can use on your own, without the help of other people. In fact, many of the ideas presented in this book are based on the premise that you can develop a broad range of self-management activities to help prevent a relapse. Many people recovering from addictions utilize all three—professional care, self-help, and self-management—at various points in their recovery.

FACTORS AFFECTING YOUR RECOVERY

Everyone's recovery journey is different and is influenced by a number of personal and environmental factors. These include:

- *The type of addiction.* Additions such as those to alcohol, drugs, or gambling require total abstinence in order for recovery to progress. Compulsive sexual behaviors and overeating are different in that the task is to stop the compulsive and self-destructive aspect of the behavior. You cannot stop eating completely if you are a compulsive overeater; whereas, if you are a cocaine addict, you do not have to keep the drug at home or even see it again. You will probably not give up sex entirely because you have a compulsive sexual disorder. Instead, you will work at eliminating the self-destructive and compulsive aspect of your sexual behaviors.

- *The severity of addiction.* There are various degrees of severity of addiction. A life that is totally consumed by an addictive illness will be different from one in which addiction does not dominate daily living. If you have had your addiction for a long time, it probably has caused many problems and complications in your life. The more severe your addiction, the more intensive your recovery program should be.

- *The presence of significant medical or psychiatric disorders.* Obesity caused by compulsive overeating, depressive illness caused by compulsive gambling, or increased anxiety and panic in the absence of alcohol use are just a few examples of medical or psychiatric disorders that can complicate your recovery. The presence of another disorder in addition to addiction may alter your recovery program. If left untreated, other illnesses can contribute to a relapse to your addiction.

- *The degree of damage that addiction has caused in your life.* The greater the damage caused to your body, mind, relationships, and lifestyle, the more challenging recovery will be. If your addiction has caused you to lose virtually everything in your life, you may feel that recovery is a constant uphill battle. Or you may feel less incentive than if you had tried to stop your addiction before significant losses occurred. Serious damage to your brain caused by long-term abuse of alcohol or drugs can impair your judgment, motivation, and, hence, your ability to recover. If your compulsive gambling or sexual addiction caused you to lose your job and spend time in jail, your recovery will face different challenges.

- *Your age.* Young people with an addiction sometimes feel cheated that they can no longer engage in their addictive behavior. Or they may feel they can take hold of the situation and learn to control their addiction because they are still young. This makes them vulnerable to relapse. Older people who have spent many years engaging in their addiction may suffer from physical or emotional problems that will make recovery more difficult.

- *Your gender.* Society is more judgmental and negative toward women with addictions than men. Women often feel more guilty and shameful than men. As a result, women may be less likely to admit that they are headed for a relapse and reach out for help and support, especially in times of high stress or difficulty.

- *Your ethnic and cultural background.* Your background is a part of who you are, how you view the world, and how you cope with personal issues or problems. Any aspect of your background can affect your recovery or contribute to a relapse. If overeating and being overweight are common in your culture and are accepted, you may feel less pressure to adhere to a recovery program that curtails overeating.

- *Your personality.* This factor plays a major role in how you deal with people and problems in life. The presence of serious personality flaws can sabotage your recovery. For example, a stubborn or self-centered person is less prone to listen to the advice of others who may offer useful suggestions for recovery and relapse prevention, just as an individual who is too dependent and insecure may come to rely too much on other people when faced with a problem. On the other hand, certain traits may enhance your recovery efforts; if you are an open person, able to listen to the advice of others or accept support from others, you are more likely to reach out for help or accept it when it's offered by someone else.

- *Your view of your addiction and the need for recovery.* If you view your addiction as life-threatening and your recovery as the way to save your dignity, or even your life, you are more likely to work hard at change. If you believe that willpower is the main way to recover, you are more than likely headed for trouble.

- *Your motivation to change.* For long-term successful recovery, your reason for getting well eventually has to come from within. However, at first it does not matter why you stop your addiction.

- *The availability of resources to support your recovery.* Access to professional treatment or self-help programs is important in getting the support you need in recovery. If you need professional care, your financial resources may significantly affect your options.

- *Your relationships with others who can support your efforts to recover.* Family or friends can be helpful and supportive. Or they can be indifferent or even hostile toward your efforts to recover. In some instances, they may sabotage your efforts on purpose.

LOSSES ASSOCIATED WITH RECOVERY

As with any major change in life, recovery from an addictive illness or disorder requires a number of adjustments. When you first start recovery, it means losing your addiction and a way of meeting your needs. Such a loss often leaves an emptiness and creates a state of internal discomfort. For many, giving up an addiction also means losing a lifestyle. Major changes in lifestyle create stress, anxiety, fear, and uncertainty. You may find, especially at first, that you don't like the sober, clean, abstinent lifestyle, that it is hard to adjust to. It is quite common to feel ambivalent—a part of you wants to give up your addiction and get well, yet another part of you also wants to hold on to it. Your feelings and desire for recovery may vary from day to day. Do not be surprised if you are highly motivated one day and do not give a damn the next.

Self-Awareness Task 2–1: *Evaluating Your Losses*

List the losses that go along with giving up your addiction.

Which of these losses is the most significant? Why?

BENEFITS OF RECOVERY

The potential benefits of recovery are endless and may relate to any area of your life. Recovery offers you the chance to regain your self-respect and dignity. Over and over, people talk about how recovery offers not only the chance to stop a self-destructive addiction, but also to improve oneself and grow as a person. It will take time before you feel some of the benefits; nonetheless, you should experience some immediate benefits as well as long-term benefits.

Self-Awareness Task 2–2: *Benefits of Recovery*

List five to ten short-term (less than six months) benefits of recovery.

List five to ten long-term (six months or longer) benefits of recovery.

Of the benefits you have already experienced, or expect to experience in the future, which is the most important? Why?

The Recovery Process

The recovery process is ongoing: recovery is never completed. It is progressive. You should try to build on your successes and take things a step at a time. Despite the many commonalities of recovery, each person has his or her own unique journey to take.

Recovery has different stages, each with its own tasks or demands to face. After you get over the initial adjustment to stopping your addiction, you will focus on learning facts about addiction and the recovery process, working through denial, making a commitment to change, and building a long-term recovery and relapse-prevention plan. You will focus your efforts mainly on resisting desires to engage in your addictive behavior, changing your lifestyle to support your recovery, and learning from your mistakes.

As recovery progresses, you will expand the focus of your efforts. You will work on increasing your self-awareness through completion of a personal inventory. You will also work at making amends for the damage caused by your addiction. You will begin to work on personal problems and issues, such as controlling your self-destructive impulses, overcoming guilt and shame, and dealing more effectively with emotions and negative thoughts.

As you get further into recovery, you will work on more lasting character and interpersonal changes. You may even reach the point at which you give to others suffering from addictions.

There is no set time at which you should be in any particular phase of recovery. The process is very individualized, and because each person is different, what fits for one may not fit for another. Some people struggle for years at working through denial and accepting their addiction. Others reach an acceptance quickly and progress to other recovery issues.

While some people have a fairly smooth road to recovery, others do not. Emotional pain is likely to be experienced as you examine your life, try to pick up the pieces, and continually work at changing yourself. No one can pretend it is easy.

How you view success is very important. You should accept that it will happen in degrees and increments, sometimes very small ones. You should strive for progress, not perfection. If you make a mistake on your recovery journey, try to learn from it. Do not use it as an excuse to give up or fall into a full-blown relapse.

RECOVERY ISSUES OR THEMES

Specific issues during recovery may vary, depending on the nature of your addiction as well as on other factors. The choice is yours whether or not you want to work on the various recovery issues. Some people choose to explore every aspect of recovery;

others limit themselves only to abstaining from the addictive behavior or to changing a few minor aspects of their lives or their character.

Most recovery issues fall into at least one of the following categories:

- *Physical.* Dealing with health problems caused by your addiction; getting sufficient exercise and rest; following a healthy diet; and having mechanisms to release stress.

- *Behavioral.* Changing behaviors unique to your addiction and lifestyle; developing new routines, habits, and coping mechanisms; stopping self-destructive behavior.

- *Cognitive.* Changing distorted beliefs and thoughts; learning to think in more positive and healthy ways; getting comfortable with the idea of being a recovering addicted person.

- *Emotional/psychological.* Working through denial of your addiction; becoming aware of your emotions; expressing positive or negative feelings when appropriate; restoring emotional stability; learning to cope with negative emotional states; changing your character defects; getting help if you have a coexisting psychiatric disorder.

- *Family.* Accepting that your addiction has affected your family members; making amends for the damage done to them; improving family relationships; getting your family involved in recovery when appropriate; changing negative aspects of your family system; respecting family members' needs for emotional distance; dealing with unresolved issues related to your original family.

- *Social.* Becoming aware of others hurt by your addiction and making amends when appropriate; developing a network of friends who support your efforts at recovery; learning how to refuse pressures to engage in your addictive behavior; developing relationships that are satisfying and mutual and that help meet your emotional and interpersonal needs; having hobbies and recreational interests that are fun and interesting.

- *Spiritual.* Accepting your limitations and flaws; learning to forgive yourself for things you have done during your addiction; reducing your feelings of guilt and shame; overcoming feelings of emptiness and gaining a purpose in your life; helping other suffering addicts; and relying on God or another higher power to give you strength to cope with difficult times.

- *Financial.* Dealing with financial problems caused by your addiction; paying back your debts for money borrowed or stolen; planning your financial future.
- *Other.* Developing goals in your life (short-, medium-, and long-range); resolving work, legal, or other problems caused by your addiction.

Some of these recovery issues will be discussed in detail in subsequent chapters in the context of long-term relapse prevention. As mentioned earlier, you may participate in professional treatment, self-help programs, and/or follow a plan of self-management. Your choice depends entirely on your circumstances and needs.

LIFESTYLE BALANCING

One of the leading experts on relapse prevention is Dr. G. Alan Marlatt of the Addictive Behaviors Research Center at the University of Washington. Dr. Marlatt has written widely about the notion that a balanced lifestyle will reduce the chances of relapse to an addiction. A balanced lifestyle is one in which your "shoulds" (or obligations) and your "wants" (desires or needs) are in some reasonable degree of balance. If you feel deprived because you have too many shoulds (obligations) in life, you may feel that returning to your addictive behavior is the only way to satisfy certain needs or desires.

In today's world, it is difficult to balance the many different demands and obligations you have. However, the more balanced your life is, the more satisfied you are likely to be and, as a result, the less susceptible you may be to relapse.

A balanced lifestyle is one in which each of the various areas of your life is attended to so that your needs are satisfied as much as possible. These areas include your physical, emotional, social, family, interpersonal, spiritual, professional, avocational, and financial functioning. In addition, you may have creative needs that must be satisfied.

Self-Awareness Task 2–3: Lifestyle Balancing

How would you describe the balance (or lack of it) in your life?

Which areas in your life do you think are out of balance? Why?

If you had to change one area of your life that is out of balance, what would it be? Describe your plan for changing this.

3

The Relapse Process

MOST people who try to kick an addiction relapse at least once. Some people relapse several times. Others continue a lifelong pattern of relapsing and become chronic relapsers.

Research conducted with people who have given up alcohol, drugs, overeating, gambling, or smoking indicates that the relapse rates are fairly similar across these various addictions. Most of the different studies show that the majority of people with an addictive disorder experience at least one relapse. A large number of these relapses happen within the first three months of recovery. However, a relapse to the addictive disorder or habit can occur at any time, even after many years of excellent recovery. Usually, though, the longer that you stay away from the addictive substance or behavior, the greater the chances that you will continue to stay away from it and do well. A lot of people say that the period of the first several months, up to a year or so, is the most difficult time in recovery. This is the time in which they feel most vulnerable to relapse.

Relapse as an Event or a Process

Relapse can be seen as an event of returning to the addictive behavior; or, it can be seen as a process in which warning signs occur indicating that you are likely to go back to your addiction if you do not take some positive steps.

The process of relapse is similar, regardless of what the specific addiction is. The following two cases show how the relapse process unfolded for a recovering alcoholic and for a sex addict.

"I caught myself just in time," says Frank, a recovering alcoholic who came close to drinking again before he realized what was happening. "I was sober for way over a year when I ran into some old buddies from high school whom I hadn't seen for years. We partied a lot back then. They invited me to a party a couple weeks down the road. About two weeks before the party I got to thinking what I should bring. After tossing it over in my mind I figured it was safe to go to the liquor store. So I went and bought a bottle of Scotch, the same kind I used to drink, mind you. But I told myself the Scotch was not for me. It was for the others at the party." During this time, Frank started missing Alcoholics Anonymous meetings. It always seemed that something more important came up. "I knew other AAs would question me about keeping liquor at home and going to a party. So I didn't say anything to them. A couple days before the party I started to question this stuff about being an alcoholic. Maybe it was all a sham and I could learn to control how much I drank. What if I at least tried it once? The party might be a good test." After going back and forth in his mind for a few days, Frank suddenly told himself he "knew damn well" he could not control his drinking. He gave his bottle of Scotch away and decided not to test himself by going to the party. Although a bit shaken up that he had come so close to drinking, Frank felt good that he had interrupted his relapse process before he actually drank.

"Just one more time," Lisa, a recovering sex addict, said to herself when she felt a very strong attraction to a man she met at a party and wanted to pick up. "I don't have to let things get out of control again. Besides, I'm feeling lonely." One of her patterns of sexually acting out before she entered a recovery program had been to frequently pick up men she had just met. An attractive, engaging woman, Lisa never had trouble finding men willing to go home with her. "My lust for men really got out of control. I went from one to the next, sometimes sleeping with two in the same day. It wasn't until I caught a disease and got beat up by a guy who was a real kook that I was forced to look at myself and what I was doing. It was like I was hooked on sex, just like a drug addict is hooked on drugs. The only difference is that they give up drugs completely. How can you give up sex completely?" Lisa's progress in recovery was up and down. The

longest she had been able to go without getting involved with strangers had been four months. "I gave in to my impulses at the party and took this guy home with me. After he left the next day I felt I really let myself down for giving in. So what did I do? Same damn thing, went out that night and found another guy."

We usually think of a relapse as an actual return to the addictive habit or behavior. However, as Frank's case shows, you can be in a relapse process *before* engaging again in addictive behavior. Or, like Lisa, you can end up actually going back to the addictive behavior. Once back, the behavior can get seriously out of control again if you do not take quick action to stop it.

Relapse simply means a process of building up that, if not responded to, is very likely to lead back to addictive use of alcohol, drugs, food, gambling, or sex, or to any other addiction from which you are recovering. In the alcohol and drug recovery field, this process is referred to as "BUD," or building up to drink (or drug) use. This building up will usually show in some type of warning sign. Such signs, which some people refer to as "red flags," may be obvious or subtle. Sometimes their presence is very apparent to other people as well as to ourselves. At other times, however, the warning signs can be subtle or even hidden from us, because behavior results from conscious as well as unconscious motivations.

Consider the following cases of two alcoholics who relapsed in a bar, each after being sober for more than ten months. Fred knew his recovery was on shaky ground and said he did not particularly like abstaining. "When I went back to my old bar, I knew it was only a matter of time before I drank again, even though I told myself I shouldn't drink. I was pretty miserable being sober." Fred actually drank the first time he went into the bar.

Jason, on the other hand, said, "I was doing well in my recovery and had no intention of drinking when I went in a bar. Everybody told me to stay clear of bars because I only had ten months' sober time. But I really believed it wouldn't happen to me, that I didn't want a drink. I just wanted to see some old buddies."

Jason made four trips to the bar before he finally ordered a drink. "When I first drank, I told myself to take it easy. Just a few beers, that's all. Funny thing is, it worked . . . but only for awhile. The problem then became my questioning whether I was really an alcoholic. Shit, if you can believe it, I started to see myself as a 'problem drinker,' not an alcoholic! I just had to exert better control over my drinking, that's all." Jason's experience is an example of a relapse "setup," which more than likely started on an unconscious level. After his first few so-called successful trips to a bar, Jason was proud of how well he had handled it. "I even began to criticize everyone who felt so negatively about me going in a bar. Thought maybe they didn't know what the hell they were talking about because I was proving them wrong. Maybe I was stronger than they were because I wasn't drinking." Jason had no conscious intention of drinking. Yet he eventually resumed drinking again. He ignored his warning signs.

Types and Effects of Relapses

There are different types and effects of relapses. On one end of the continuum are "therapeutic relapses," which help the person become more motivated to pursue a stronger recovery program. This type of relapse frequently shakes up the person who experiences it, who often believes that he or she is doing so well in recovery that relapse is very unlikely to occur. Jerry, a compulsive overeater, lost 130 pounds as he diligently worked on a recovery program. He went to Overeaters Anonymous meetings as well as seeing a therapist. After almost two years of doing very well, he began to let up on his recovery program and believed that he would never go back to the way he had been before. Consequently, Jerry began exercising less frequently and started eating some of the junk food that he had given up. Jerry began to feel guilty and like a failure, so at first he chose not to talk about his relapse. Quickly, Jerry put on 22 pounds. He soon realized, however, that he was slipping back. Shocked though he was that it had happened to him, he used this relapse experience to motivate himself to work harder. He made a point of resuming his regular exercise regimen, abstaining from junk food, and talking about his experiences with other men and women in the

Overeaters Anonymous program. It was an excellent lesson for Jerry to learn that he was not invulnerable. His relapse helped him in the long run because it made him realize that he was not a special case, not exempt from relapse.

On the other end of the continuum are fatal relapses. Some alcoholics and drug addicts, for example, end up dying from accidents, overdoses, suicides, or medical complications caused by returning to substance abuse. I remember one young alcoholic, drug addicted man who slowly had begun to put his life together following a rather extensive history of addiction and criminal behavior. After one of his relapses, he acted wildly and jumped into a river with a bottle of whiskey in his hand. His impaired judgment led him to show off to a group of people by jumping into the very deep river with his clothes on. He was definitely too drunk to know that he could not handle the strong current or the deep waters of the river. He paid with his life.

In between the extremes of therapeutic and fatal relapses are other types with serious, moderate, or mild consequences. The following cases show examples from several different types of addictions.

- Betty, a forty-one-year-old recovering compulsive overeater, went on a two-month eating binge that started in the Christmas holidays. Not only did she regain thirty-seven pounds, but her blood pressure skyrocketed. She also experienced a serious episode of depression. She and her husband argued over her relapse.

- Jim, a forty-nine-year-old alcoholic with twenty-four years working for the same company, lost his job following his third relapse. Jim missed many days of work, was often late, and once was caught drinking on the job. His boss felt that Jim had had enough chances and was costing the company money.

- Lamont, a twenty-eight-year-old drug addict, relapsed after receiving a pain medication following dental work. Lamont's desire for drugs was reawakened, and to get pain pills he began cashing in forged prescriptions. Because he was on parole, this violation cost him his freedom, as he was sent back to prison. His seven-year-old son was heartbroken to lose his father again.

- Diane, a fifty-one-year-old teacher addicted to gambling, began buying lottery tickets. She then withdrew eight hundred dollars from her savings account and took a weekend trip to a gambling casino, despite strong objections from her husband. Even though she won a sum of money, when she returned she realized that she was falling back into her addiction. With the support of her husband and therapist, she took hold of herself and stopped her relapse before it got out of hand.

- Al, a forty-one-year-old electrician who is a recovering sex addict, did well for over one year. He stopped seeing prostitutes, picking up women, masturbating compulsively, and reading pornography. One week, when his wife and children were away visiting her parents, Al bought several pornographic magazines and rented a videotape. After masturbating several times during the weekend, Al went cruising for women. When he could not hustle one, he picked up a prostitute. Later, his wife accidently found the magazines when cleaning the house. A very heated argument ensued, during which she expressed her disappointment, anger, and fear. She told Al she would not put up with him if he returned to his compulsive sexual behaviors. Al got very angry in return and told himself that he deserved another woman for putting up with his nagging wife. "I'll show her," he thought to himself as he started planning how to pick up a sexual partner. He soon came to his senses, however, and called his sponsor in Sex and Love Addicts Anonymous. After several lengthy discussions with him, Al apologized to his wife and told her he could understand why she was upset. Al told her that he and his sponsor had agreed on a plan to stop his relapse from continuing and then asked her for support in getting over this rough period. Al asked his wife to share her feelings and reactions to what had happened and for any ideas she had for helping him return to the right track.

These cases clearly show that relapses vary significantly in terms of their consequences and effects. Usually, the more quickly you can take action to interrupt a relapse, the less damage is done. All relapses have potentially serious consequences and it is not always possible to predict how a relapse will turn out. Even if you think a relapse is "no big deal," it certainly can turn out to be a big deal.

Relapse Warning Signs

As mentioned earlier, the process of relapse shows in clues or warning signs that may be obvious or subtle. Sometimes these signs are in your conscious awareness and you can clearly see them, even if you do not do anything about them. At other times, warning signs are not in your conscious awareness. Other people may notice these signs long before you do. Denial can be the force behind a failure to see these clues to relapse.

Warning signs may occur hours, days, weeks, or even months before a return to an addictive behavior. Relapse sometimes happens impulsively, but for the majority of people actively working with a program of recovery from an addiction relapse will usually occur gradually. Even when you see warning signs and have every intention of not engaging in the addictive habit, the relapse process still may evolve slowly. For example, Gene, an alcoholic who had been sober for over five years, built up to a drunken episode over a period of several months. Prior to giving in to his desire to drink, which he had wrestled with for many weeks, he had made four trips to a liquor store before finally buying a bottle of booze. The time between first going to the liquor store and at last buying the booze was over four weeks.

Signs of the relapse process usually show up internally in attitudes, thoughts, or feelings. Or they may show up externally in behaviors or actions. People usually experience a combination of these signs as part of the relapse process. Some relatively common signs are associated with different types of addiction; however, usually each person will have some warning signs that are unique to his or her situation.

While you do not want to interpret any change that you experience as indicative of being in a relapse process, your recovery can be greatly aided by paying attention to changes that occur in your attitudes, thoughts, moods, or behaviors. In this way you can reach some conclusions about whether or not the changes signal the relapse process. The following cases show examples of changes preceding relapses by several addicted individuals who were involved in a recovery program.

Attitude changes. Ann, a compulsive overeater, stopped caring about her recovery. "I just didn't give a damn anymore. It was such a hassle, I just quit caring." Negative attitudes about life in general, or about recovery in particular, may indicate a relapse process. Such attitudes often negatively affect the motivation to change. "Why bother?" "I just don't care," and "The effort isn't worth it" are commonly experienced attitudes.

Changes in thinking. After eighteen months of recovery, Dave, a sex addict, said, "I started believing that I was cured, that my addiction was finally under control. Then, after working extremely hard for several months on a project at work, I thought that I deserved a reward. And, what better way to reward myself than saying it was OK to pick up a woman for a good time? It would be different this time!" Addictive thinking is hard to change and can return even during periods in which you do not engage in the addictive habit. Old thought patterns are not easy to get rid of.

Changes in behavior. "I stopped over to see my old bookie to see if I could get tickets to the football game," said Neil, an addictive gambler. "Yeah, even though I told myself I wouldn't place no bets, I let him talk me into it." The most frequently cited behaviors related to the relapse process include returning to places or contacting people associated with the addictive habit; cutting down on or completely stopping therapy sessions or self-help group meetings without a good justification or a discussion of the decision with someone who understands addiction; and showing an increase in stress symptoms, such as smoking or eating more, feeling restless or anxious, or having trouble sleeping or relaxing.

Mood changes. "Before I went on an eating binge," said Marie, a compulsive overeater, "I became increasingly depressed. I felt my life was going downhill. Rather than continue feeling so awfully depressed, I pigged out. Binging helped—at first, but I always felt more depressed after I was done eating and thought about what I did to myself. And, the more depressed I felt, the more I ate. What a vicious cycle!" Strong negative feelings such as depression, anxiety, anger, or boredom, as well as strong positive feelings such as excitement or euphoria often are a part of a relapse process. They occur long before the first drink, drug, bet, or other addictive substance or behavior.

One of the leading experts on relapse prevention, Dr. G. Alan Marlatt, has written about this process as a "relapse chain." Each relapse warning sign or clue can be seen as one link in this relapse chain. Each link represents an event or situation in which we make a decision that in one way or another affects relapse or recovery. According to Dr. Marlatt, we make "apparently-irrelevant-decisions" that, at the time they are made, seem to have little to do with our recovery or a potential relapse, but in reality have a great deal to do with it. Consider one addict's experiences that illustrate this kind of decision.

Ron is a thirty-six-year-old businessman with a history of alcoholism, cocaine addiction, and compulsive gambling. While driving in their car with his wife on vacation, he came to a sign indicating that Lake Tahoe was in one direction and that his chosen vacation spot was in another. It was a pretty day so he suggested to his wife that they take the long way to their vacation site by driving through Lake Tahoe so that they could enjoy the lovely sights along the way. When they arrived at Tahoe, it was lunch time, so Ron suggested that they stop for something to eat. He chose a restaurant in one of the casinos that he said had great food. After lunch, he told his wife that, as they were there, they might as well have a look at the casino. In no time, he was gambling again, much to the dismay of his wife. He promised his wife profusely that he would limit how much he would gamble and assured her that they would leave by dinner time so that they could reach their destination by late evening.

Ron made several "apparently-irrelevant-decisions" without being aware of most of them. The first link in his relapse chain probably was when he decided to vacation in a spot not far from Lake Tahoe. Other links included the decision to drive to Lake Tahoe and to eat lunch in a gambling casino's restaurant. Ron had no conscious intention of gambling until after he had lunch. Yet his decision up to that point greatly influenced his relapse.

Figure 3–1 gives a graphic way to look at this relapse process. The recovery process is represented by a road. Usually, prior to reaching the "relapse fork" in the road, many things happen over a period of time to give the addict an indication that the addictive behavior is about to be engaged in again. Once the addict lapses and initially engages in the addictive behavior, he or she may go down different paths: the path to a full-blown relapse or the path back to recovery.

Learning from Your Past Relapses

If you have relapsed before, take time to review your past warning signs. You can identify your past warning signs and the circumstances surrounding your relapse by tracing it backward, starting at the point at which you first engaged in your addictive behavior. Talking about this with someone you trust, such as a sponsor in a self-help program, another recovering addict, a therapist, or a close relative or friend may also help.

You can evaluate your relapse by answering the following questions:

When did you relapse (time, day, season of the year)?

How did you react when you first engaged in the addictive behavior again (that is, took the first drink, bet, and so on)?

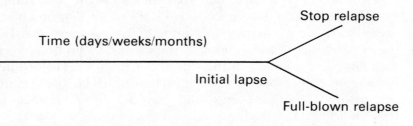

Relapse Warning Signs
- attitude changes
- behavior changes
- mood/emotional state changes
- thought changes

Figure 3–1. The Relapse Process

How long did your relapse go on (that is, how long did you use addictive substances or engage in other addictive behaviors)?

Whom were you with?

Where did your relapse occur?

What attitude changes preceded your relapse?

What thought changes preceded your relapse?

What changes in emotions preceded your relapse?

What changes in behaviors preceded your relapse?

How much time elapsed between the emergence of the clues and your involvement in the addictive behavior?

What did you learn from your relapse experience?

What will you do differently in the future when relapse warning signs show?

If you have relapsed many times, focus on the most recent ones to see if there are any patterns or similarities between your relapses in terms of when and where they occurred, or whom you were with. Were the circumstances or warning signs alike in any way? The best you can do is to learn from your past mistakes and try to do things differently so that you don't repeat the mistakes.

If you have never relapsed, learn from others who have by listening to their descriptions of their warning signs and experiences. You will see that, despite individual differences, some commonalities are often experienced by those who relapse. You can also learn about these common warning signs by reading pamphlets or books written by experts on relapse (see the bibliography at the end of this book).

RECOVERY/RELAPSE CALENDAR

One way to graphically portray your history of recovery and relapses is to complete a calendar using a green pen to indicate periods of recovery, and a red pen to indicate periods of relapse.

Take a sheet of paper and write the twelve months of the year across the top of the page, beginning with January on the left side of the paper and working toward the right. Leave some room on the left margin and write in the past five to ten years, one year at a time. To the best of your memory go back over your history of recovery, starting with the present year and working backward. For the periods in which you were in recovery and not engaging in your addictive behavior, make a line in green. For the periods in which you were engaging in your addictive behavior, make a line in red. The actual lines you make may be for less than a month, or for several months, or even longer.

After you make this calendar, very slowly take a close look at it to see if any patterns exist. What do the different colored lines tell you about your history of recovery and/or relapse? Are your periods of recovery getting longer? Or shorter? Are relapses occurring at similar times of the year? If so, why? What could be causing you to go back to your addiction at the same times of the year?

RESULTS OF A LAPSE/RELAPSE

As you think back over any relapse experience(s), focus on the initial lapse, or first time you went back to your addictive behavior. What did you think, feel, or do after this lapse occurred? How did you view yourself as an addicted and/or recovering person? For example, did you tell yourself you were a failure, unmotivated, or incapable of recovering? Because you made a mistake, did you justify a full-blown relapse? How did others— your family, sponsor, or recovery friends—react to and view your relapse? What, if anything, did they say to you, and how did this affect you?

The response to the initial lapse is very important because it often dictates what to do next. The following cases illustrate two entirely different responses to the initial lapse. Nancy cut hers off quickly, while Jack continued and caused himself serious problems.

Nancy, a twenty-eight-year-old dietician, is a compulsive over-eater who forces herself to vomit after eating to avoid gaining weight. During the first nine months of her recovery she did well and did not have any episodes of compulsive overeating or purging herself. "After an argument with my boyfriend I became quite upset and angry. I felt he didn't understand me or care about me. Feeling very sorry for myself, I went on a sweet shopping spree, buying my favorite chocolate candy, a few dozen cookies, and a scrumptious mocha cake. I binged just once, then made myself throw up. Fortunately, I quickly realized this was no way to deal with my feelings. So I gave the rest of the sweets to my neighbors. Then, I called my boyfriend and told him I wanted to talk things out. We worked things out. While I felt bad I binged and purged again, I felt good for not letting it get out of hand.

Jack, a truck driver with a long history of addictive gambling, finally got help when his wife threatened him. "You gotta stop this gambling nonsense or get your ass out of the house. You ain't nothing but trouble lately, blowing your money while me and the kids do without stuff." Jack reluctantly gave in to her and stopped "serious" gambling such as high stakes poker games and betting with bookies on sporting events. He even went to a few Gamblers Anonymous meetings and began identifying with other compulsive gamblers. However, Jack said, "I still dabbled in the lottery, buying five or ten bucks worth of tickets every day. I didn't think it was no big deal, not real gambling like betting on games or playing poker." After several weeks of buying lottery tickets, Jack won a large amount of money, much more than a thousand dollars. "It got me fired up. Started me thinking about winning some more money. So I called my bookie and placed bets on baseball games. Wouldn't you know, I won some more. Man, I was on a roll. Yeah, I got greedy. I wanted to win big one more time, then maybe I'd give it up for good. In a week's time, I lost all this dough. I had a lucky feeling so I cashed in the kids' savings bonds and lost all that. Then, I called my wife one Saturday and lied through my teeth. Told her the car broke down and I needed a couple hundred bucks to get it fixed. I actually left it at a friend's house and borrowed his car. Well, my wife fell for my con, but I blew that money too. Things kept snowballing. To make a long story short, my wife reached her limit with me when the phone was cut off because I gambled the money to pay the phone bill away. She kicked my ass out. Ya couldn't really blame her after the shit I put her through."

Developing an Action Plan for Dealing with Relapse Warning Signs

Taking a proactive approach by developing an action plan for dealing with relapse warning signs puts you in the position of feeling a greater sense of control over your options. It also reduces the chances that you will be taken by surprise by a possible relapse. Each of the steps in developing a relapse-prevention plan is discussed below.

Step 1: Be aware of relapse warning signs. This step was discussed in detail in the previous sections, so only a brief review is in order here. A major aspect of the journey of recovery is awareness that potential roadblocks, potholes, or detours exist. As mentioned before, this awareness of warning signs comes from several sources:

1. your own past relapse experiences, particularly the warning signs that showed before you returned to your addictive habit;
2. the relapse experiences of other recovering addicted people; and
3. informational recovery guides written specifically on the topic of relapse.

The latter two sources will help you learn about the common relapse warning signs that seem to occur frequently with many different people suffering from various types of addictive disorders.

Step 2: Develop a written action plan. This written plan should specifically list the various warning signs that you identified. It should include a variety of ways you can cope with each warning sign rather than just one strategy. This is in case the strategy you try to use does not work at a given time.

You can use different types of strategies in developing your action plan. One is developing general strategies that may help regardless of the specific warning sign. General strategies include such things as calling your sponsor or another recovering member of the self-help program you are in; going to a self-help meeting; or calling your therapist if you are in counseling.

Specific strategies relate to a particular relapse warning sign. Say, for example, that your sign is a significant increase in thoughts about going back to your addictive habit and enjoying the high it brought you. You may deal with this by reflecting, asking yourself why these thoughts have increased at this time, and trying to figure out where they are coming from. You could tell yourself, "It's one thing to have these thoughts, but another thing entirely to act on them. I'll wait a couple of days before I even consider acting on them." By this time, the thoughts may have gone or you may have figured out other ways to cope with them. Or you could review what your addiction did to your life and what benefits recovery has brought to you and to your family.

Coping strategies may involve leaning on others for support or working things out within yourself. Usually it is helpful to develop both types because you cannot always lean on others and you cannot always work things out by yourself.

Step 3: Discuss your plan with another person. Reviewing your written plan with a trusted friend, sponsor, other recovering person, or family member will give you the chance to get feedback from others. This will help you determine if your coping strategies are reasonable and can be easily implemented. You may also get additional ideas on ways to cope with warning signs, especially from other recovering addicts who have experienced them in the past.

Step 4: Implement your action plan. Easier said than done! Many addicted people do a splendid job of identifying warning signs and devising excellent action plans, only to fail to follow through. Remember, talk is cheap. Recovery plans have to be translated into action. Regardless of what you say you will do, recovery comes down to your concrete actions and behaviors.

One way to prepare yourself is to make a list of all the barriers you might create to prevent implementing your action plans. Then, ask yourself why you created them. Naturally, many of us do not want to change, especially when a lot of effort and hard work is involved. Doing things the old way, or the easy way, seems a great deal easier.

Failure to translate your strategies from a plan to action may result from several things. It can reflect denial of your problem. Or it can mean that your motivation is questionable. It may also indicate that your coping strategies are not achievable.

You can also practice your new coping strategies before you actually try them out during a real relapse process. This gives you a chance to work out potential problems. It also helps you be more realistic about how relapse warning signs may actually affect you and about what strategies may work.

CASE EXAMPLE

Mary, recovering from compulsive overeating, tells how she put her action plan to work.

"A major part of my relapse [prevention] process was dealing with my anger in ways that were direct and healthy. In the past, I kept my anger inside and let it build up. This would always justify an eating binge. I knew this had to stop if I were to prevent a relapse. Like a lot of people, I knew in my head all the things a person could do to express anger. It was so hard for me, but I did it. I first had to practice it in my head. I would imagine telling other people how I felt and how they would respond. At first, I backed down even when expressing anger in my imagination. Gradually, I became more comfortable imagining myself talking directly to others. I also practiced expressing my feelings by making statements to the mirror. This allowed me to work on my facial expressions, tone of voice, and the words I chose. I also arranged practice sessions with another person who would play the role of the person towards whom I felt angry. Sure it wasn't easy, but in time I got more and more comfortable. The real clincher was that when I actually used this stuff in my real life it worked much easier than I would ever have imagined. I found out that most people will listen to you when you tell them you're upset. You feel better about yourself. And, you get more respect from others because often they don't even know they've done anything that you felt upset about. The real key to my success was practice because it built my confidence up and made me feel less nervous about confronting other people.

4

High-Risk Relapse Factors

WHY do people go back to addictive habits or behaviors after a period of recovery, especially if their addictions had caused considerable harm to them or to their families? A drug addict who had nearly died on several occasions from drug overdoses, had lost a job and a family, and had gone to jail because of the addiction would be considered crazy for returning to drugs again. A compulsive overeater who had developed serious medical problems from significant weight gains and had become suicidally depressed because of this also would seem crazy for binging on food again. A sex addict who had experienced private despair and public humiliation, and whose family was shamed would similarly be out of his mind to engage in the sexual addiction again. Right?

Why would someone go back to an addictive habit or behavior if recovery had brought many rewards? An alcoholic whose recovery helped save his family, job, and dignity would be out of his mind to drink again. A compulsive gambler who let go of his private despair, overcame serious depression and thoughts of suicide, and worked himself out of deep debt would also be out of his mind to stop his recovery program and gamble again. Right?

But relapse, like addiction itself, sometimes simply defies logic. Because of this, addictive disorders are often referred to as baffling and cunning. The cunning aspect shows in relapse. Any discussion of an addictive disorder has to take into account the possibility of relapse, which, as mentioned in earlier chapters, happens to the majority of those trying to kick an addiction.

Over a decade ago, a leading researcher on addiction relapse, Dr. G. Alan Marlatt, introduced the concept of high-risk factors. According to Dr. Marlatt, each addict has high-risk factors that make him or her vulnerable to a future relapse if the addict does not prepare to handle these factors. Dr. Marlatt and his colleagues have categorized these relapse risk factors according to how common they are with various addictions. Although certainly there are differences among the relapse risk factors with various addictions, there are a lot of similarities as well. An important fact shown in Dr. Marlatt's work is that identifying high-risk relapse factors and learning coping strategies are essential for recovery.

Dr. Helen Annis is a leading researcher at the Addictions Research Foundation in Ontario, Canada. She has found that the situations in which alcoholics and drug addicts used heavily during the year prior to treatment are most likely to be the situations in which they use alcohol or drugs in the future. So, if you drank when you were depressed before you got treatment, depression in the future may represent a high-risk relapse factor for you. It is very probable that this idea can apply to other types of addiction as well, not just alcoholism and drug addiction. Dr. Annis also found that confidence level is an important variable in relapse. The more confident you are that you can handle a high-risk factor without engaging in your addictive behavior, the more likely you are to succeed. However, there are cases in which you can get overconfident and put yourself in situations in which you are very likely to relapse. This is sometimes a "relapse setup."

High-risk factors usually fall into one of two major types: (1) internal, such as thoughts, feelings, desires, or urges and cravings, and (2) external, such as relationships, events, activities, places, and even certain material things or objects. Regardless of the addiction, all addicted people have a variety of internal and external risk factors. Knowing what these are, what causes them, how they show in your thoughts and physical symptoms, and how they affect your behavior, can help you better prepare for how to handle them. Remember, it is not just the risk factor, but what you do with it that determines whether or not you actually relapse. Your ability to cope with it is what finally determines whether or not you will relapse.

Knowing Your High-Risk Relapse Factors

You can identify your relapse risk factors in several ways. One way is to make a list of the situations in which you engaged in your addictive habit or behavior in the past. Once you complete this list, you can then prioritize it, listing the situations in order from the greatest potential risk to your recovery to the least. The biggest risk factor, for example, would be listed first, followed by the other ones.

A second way to determine your relapse risk factors is to think about all the internal feelings, external situations, people, places, and things associated with your addiction. Make a list of all these associations, no matter how insignificant some of them may seem.

A third way you can identify your personal risk factors is to review lists of common risk factors devised by researchers or therapists. For example, in my *Relapse Prevention Workbook* I list sixty of the most common high-risk situations for alcoholics and drug addicts. Dr. Annis has devised an "Inventory of Drinking Situations" and an "Inventory of Drug-Taking Situations" that can help an alcoholic or drug addict identify high-risk factors. You may be able to adapt these lists of high-risk factors to your particular addiction by substituting compulsive sex, gambling, or overeating for alcohol or drugs.

A fourth way is for you to have a relapse fantasy in which you imagine going back to your addiction. Where and when does this occur in your fantasy? Whom are you with? What are the circumstances surrounding your relapse? What do you think and feel as you engage in your addiction in this fantasy? How does it end?

A fifth way is to discuss any dreams you have in which you engage in your addiction. You can answer the same questions as in the previous paragraph on relapse fantasies.

If you have actually relapsed in the past, writing a relapse autobiography is another way of helping pinpoint high-risk relapse factors. This autobiography should cover everything you remember about your relapse: what behavior(s) it involved, how long it went on, when and where it occurred, what led up to it, why it happened, what warning signs were present before you relapsed, who else, if anyone, was involved, and how it ended.

A final way is to note which of the relapse risk factors discussed in the remainder of this chapter relate to your situation. Identify the high-risk factors that seem to characterize your situation the best. The list that follows is based on a review of research, clinical and self-help writings, and my experience working with addicts for over a decade. Although it is comprehensive, there may be factors that you consider to be high-risk that are not mentioned.

High-risk factors are listed separately for purposes of discussion, but in reality they usually occur in combination. Even though it is impossible to cover all high-risk factors, the following sections present the most common ones.

NEGATIVE EMOTIONAL STATES

Negative feelings or emotional states were the number one relapse risk factor among a large group of addicts studied by G. Alan Marlatt and other researchers at the University of Washington's Addiction Research Center. Negative mood states were a factor in relapses for 47 percent of gamblers, 38 percent of alcoholics, 37 percent of smokers, 33 percent of overeaters, and 19 percent of heroin addicts in the study. Several other researchers and therapists have reported that depression and anxiety were major factors in a substantial number of relapses. Following is a brief discussion of the numerous negative emotional states that may contribute to an addict's relapse.

Anger. Issues of anger are constantly brought up by addicts in professional treatment as well as in self-help group meetings. If one emotional state stands out as more common or problematic than others, it has to be anger. Indeed, the acronym HALT, used in self-help programs, stands for not getting too hungry, angry, lonely, or tired, as these feelings can contribute to a relapse.

For many addicted people, the problem is with angry feelings and what to do with them. Often, anger is dealt with in one of two extreme ways: it is acted on impulsively and aggressively, without regard to consequences, in order to release it or express it; or it is held in and suppressed so that it slowly builds up and the person seethes on the inside. When the latter occurs, it is not unusual to engage in the addictive habit or behavior for temporary relief or even for revenge.

For some addicts, the problem is a negative personality trait that shows up as chronic anger. This type of person gets angry very easily, often for no valid reason. Angry people are the ones most likely to show this trait. It really does not matter what someone does or says to them—they are programmed to get angry a lot. No reason is really needed. The problem is, however, that they do not recognize this trait and typically blame everyone else for their feelings or problems.

Anxiety. Feelings of anxiety are fairly common when you first give up an addiction. These feelings stem from the psychological adjustments caused by making such a major change as stopping an addictive habit or behavior. People worry a lot about what it will be like to live without their addictive habit, whether they can "stay stopped," and other things that such a major life change will bring. Or perhaps the addictive habit is one way of controlling anxious feelings.

With some addictions, such as to alcohol or other drugs, anxiety can also be caused by the physiological effects of stopping chemical use. Withdrawal may produce this anxiety. In fact, withdrawal can even be protracted, with the body taking weeks or longer to adjust to being chemically free. In these cases, anxiety may linger.

The first weeks and months of change typically are the most anxiety-provoking. In some instances, anxiety is persistent and cannot easily be shaken. It shows in shakiness, jitteriness, jumpiness, feeling tense, edginess, tiredness, or inability to relax. Physical symptoms such as sweating, a pounding heart, stomach distress, or dizziness often accompany such anxiety. The person with this type of more serious anxiety worries a lot, turns things over and over in his or her mind, and often expects bad things to happen. This type of anxiety usually represents a psychiatric illness that requires specialized treatment, because it will not necessarily go away on its own. It is not unusual for very anxious people to turn to liquor or tranquilizers to calm down their anxiety.

How we think affects how we feel. Anxiety, like other emotional states, can have its roots in our thinking. We talk ourselves into worrying and feeling anxious. Sometimes, the idea of doing something is much more anxiety-provoking than the reality of it. This is called "anticipatory anxiety." A common example of this is when you have to speak in front of a group of people. Thinking about doing this and about how the people will see you and respond to you often is much more anxiety-provoking than actually having to make the speech. Mark Twain expressed this best when he said, "I am an old man and have known many troubles, but most of them *never* happened!"

Boredom. A significant relapse factor for many, boredom often accompanies a major life change in which people give up something, such as an addiction, that has played a big part in their lives. Whatever the negative aspects of addiction, it often provides a structure for people's lives. Excitement is frequently associated with thinking about or planning how to engage in an addiction. For example, Mike, a sex addict, said, "Planning where I was going to try to pick up a woman, then cruising around was a high for me. It got my adrenaline flowing. It was all part of my sickness." Many gamblers report a similar feeling of excitement when they study racing odds, figure out point spreads for ball games, or decide which gaming tables to visit at casinos and how they are going to win. Drug addicts—particularly those addicted to cocaine, speed, or other stimulant drugs—report feeling excited before obtaining drugs as well as after they use them. Some people involved in deviant activities such as selling drugs or an addictive lifestyle experience a certain degree of excitement from this as well. Naturally, someone who gives up an addiction loses other highs associated with it. The result is frequently boredom. Sobriety from addiction does not seem nearly as exciting as engaging in the addiction, especially at first. And, to top things off, recovering addicts are expected to make a lot of other changes as well.

Some people have a character trait that shows in needing a high level of activity or excitement. It is as if such people cannot stand to slow down. Their threshold for pleasure is quite high.

They feel bored if they are not always doing something or involved in multiple projects. And it is not unusual for this to show as a need to be part of risky or dangerous activities.

Boredom may also occur if you are not able to structure your time or fill your days with meaningful or enjoyable activities. It is common, for example, for addicts early in recovery to find themselves with a lot of empty time that used to be spent in the addiction. What to do with this time is a problem for many and boredom and restlessness result.

Boredom with jobs or relationships can occur when you give up an addictive habit. Perhaps the addiction made undesirable situations tolerable. Or it may be that when the addiction is stripped away—particularly alcoholism and drug addiction—you more clearly notice things that you did not see before or give a damn about because of being affected by chemicals.

Regardless of the type or cause of boredom, it can trigger a relapse to addictive behavior. Boredom is something to pay attention to.

Depression. Many addicts report feelings of depression. These feelings may stem from the physiological effects of addictive substances such as alcohol or other drugs. Or depression may come from the social, family, financial, spiritual, or legal effects of addiction. Losses often result from addiction: jobs, money, status, relationships, dignity, and self-esteem. For some, loss of addiction represents the loss of a lifestyle. Many talk about losing an addiction as being similar to losing a good friend because, despite any damage it caused, the addiction also provided something to the addict.

Feelings of depression can be much more serious than the blues that everyone experiences now and then. These feelings can be a symptom of a depressive illness. With this type of depression also come feelings of hopelessness, helplessness, and guilt. Other symptoms that go along with depression are problems concentrating, decreased energy, loss of interest or pleasure in usual activities, sleep or appetite disturbance, and thoughts, plans, or attempts at suicide.

Studies of alcoholics and drug addicts, for example, indicate fairly high rates of depression. While a large percentage represents organic depression caused by alcohol or drug use, a sizable number of addicts continue to experience depression long after chemical use has stopped. Sometimes a depressive illness can begin long after the addiction has stopped. There are different types of depressive illnesses with a variety of causes. Difficult, stressful, or very painful life events such as the death of a loved one or a broken marriage can trigger depression.

Negative or depressive thoughts can contribute to this illness as well. Experts such as Dr. Aaron Beck and Dr. David Burns have written extensively about their research and clinical work. They suggest that certain styles of pessimistic or negative thinking can alter your mood and contribute to depression.

Medical illnesses or taking certain types of medications can play a role in the development of depression. And there are some instances in which depression appears to stem from biological forces that have little to do with what happens in a person's life. Depression, like many types of addiction, tends to run in families, and depression rates among addicts are higher than for the general population.

An addict may return to the addictive habit or behavior as a way of coping with depression. Even if a relapse is costly in the long run, the prospect of getting some relief for depression, especially quick relief, can cause a lapse. Depression can affect relapse indirectly when it takes away the energy or motivation to participate in recovery activities. Julia, a recovering overeater, got very depressed for about seven weeks. As her depression worsened, she lost interest in Overeaters Anonymous meetings and eventually stopped going to them completely. Letting up on her program was directly related to her depression. As a result she convinced herself that a food binge might cheer her up. Oddly enough, on another level, she knew that she would probably feel worse for relapsing. At the time of her decision, however, she was attempting to help herself feel better.

Emptiness. Removing an addiction leads to an empty space that needs to be filled with something of importance. This task certainly is easier said than done. "When I stopped gambling I felt lost," said Kay, long addicted to a variety of gambling behaviors. "I felt part of me was missing. Like I was empty. What did I have to do now? Gambling was such a big part of me." What Kay was talking about was a lack of meaning or purpose, or an emptiness in which little mattered to her. Addicts often refer to this as feeling a void. Some describe this as spiritual bankruptcy.

If addictive sexual behavior gave structure and meaning to an individual's life, another purpose must replace this behavior when it is stopped. Sometimes the feeling of emptiness may occur because important spiritual beliefs and practices were lost along the road of addiction. Losing important relationships, roles, or activities can be a factor as well.

Fear/Phobia. Most of us are afraid of one thing or another in life. However, when a fear becomes irrational and leads to avoiding objects or situations, it is considered a phobia. Fears of such things as going out of the home, being closed in, or speaking in public are a source of great personal distress and interfere with getting along in life for some people. It is not unusual for alcoholics or drug addicts to seek relief from fears or phobias through liquor or tranquilizers. Therefore phobias that are not treated with the proper type of psychiatric or psychological treatment can be a risk factor for some people.

Guilt. This is a bad feeling that stems from our thoughts, actions, or behaviors. It is impossible to have an addictive habit and not do or say things that bring pain to others. Or perhaps we bring pain to ourselves. Whatever the circumstance, the result can be the same: excessive guilt.

Stan's sexual addiction wreaked havoc on his family. He gave his wife a venereal disease, spent considerable sums of money on pornography and prostitutes, and was often so busy satisfying his sexual appetite that he spent little time with his three children. "I lied through my teeth many times to try to cover my actions," he said. "I was a very busy professional so it was easy to create stories leading my family to believe I had some important project that demanded most of my time. And," Stan said, "this was just the tip of the iceberg. There were lots of other things I did, as well as some things I didn't do." As Stan reviewed these and similar actions, he was overcome with tremendous feelings of guilt because he knew what he had done had hurt so many others. In the early weeks of his recovery, he experienced many surges of guilt as he thought back on these things. Stan also felt guilty when he experienced strong fantasies of sex with other partners.

At this point in his recovery, Stan did not fully understand the difference between thoughts and actions. The result was that he judged himself harshly and was tempted to get involved in sexual activities that once were part of his addiction in order to temporarily escape from his guilt.

Hatred. Intense feelings of hatred are experienced by some addicts, especially victims of recurrent physical, sexual, or emotional abuse. Extreme hurt usually lies under such feelings of hatred. Stopping an addiction quite frequently opens up awareness of inner feelings as people explore their life experiences. When you no longer have the addictive habit to "protect" you from your feelings sometimes they surface and overwhelm you as you begin your recovery journey.

I have conducted many groups for adult children who had an addicted parent or caretaker while growing up. Some of the stories shared have been horrible, and the examples of mistreatment are unending. David, a young drug addict, gave numerous examples of mistreatment by his alcoholic father. The more he shared, the more visibly upset he became, and he broke into tears at one point. David felt that his father's alcoholism had destroyed his childhood, not to mention his whole family. His father tragically died from cirrhosis of the liver. David never had a chance to make peace with him and was left with awful memories and bad feelings. When a group member asked him what he wanted to do with his strong feelings of hatred, David blurted out, "I want to go piss on my father's grave. I hate his fucking guts for what he did." David's hatred was so deep and tormenting that he constantly went back to getting high on drugs. He knew it was an excuse, but he said he did not know how else to stop his emotional pain. It was not until he learned to let go of his hatred that he was able to stop his relapses.

Hopelessness. One of the worst feelings is hopelessness, the feeling that things will never get better, that you are destined to suffer forever. Commonly, this feeling may be strong at first, especially if your addiction has caused serious harm to you or others. Persistent feelings of hopelessness that do not go away as recovery progresses are usually connected to a depressive illness.

Many addicts have struggled for many years with their recovery and from one relapse to the next. Even with substantial recovery time between relapses, such a pattern leads to questioning whether they are able to, or capable of, getting well and overcoming the addiction. This results in feeling hopeless.

Joylessness. Lack of joy in life can be a potent relapse risk factor. Fred Zackon, an expert in treating drug addicts, sees relapses as understandable acts of satisfaction-seeking. Even though these acts are self-destructive, they at least provide the addict with a temporary respite from misery. According to Zackon, there are few sources of pleasure during early abstinence. An absence in joy results. The things that bring a sense of joy or pleasure to nonaddicts—a loving relationship, an important hobby or job, participation in a pleasurable activity, and so forth—often do not bring joy to addicts. Addicts have lost, or perhaps never had, the ability to enjoy pleasure in the simple things in life. Going back to an addiction seems far preferable to lacking a sense of joy in life.

Loneliness. Remember HALT, the acronym advising recovering addicts to not get too hungry, angry, lonely, or tired because these feelings increase vulnerability to relapse? A common side effect of addiction is lost relationships. Many marriages, close relationships, and friendships end because of the problems created by an addictive habit or disorder. Although lost relationships sometimes can be regained, often they are permanently lost. Some addicts relate mainly to other addicts, thus limiting their circle of friends. When addicts enter recovery, they often cut loose from old friends, particularly those with whom they shared the addictive behavior. Such losses contribute to a sense of isolation or loneliness.

Panic. Panic refers to attacks of intense fears or terrors, which are often associated with feelings of impending doom. The person may even feel like he or she is going to die or go crazy. Sweating, faintness, shaking, chest pain or discomfort, choking or smothering sensations, dizziness, hot and cold flashes, or tingling in the hands or feet are physical symptoms that appear during panic attacks. "Something awful is going to happen" is a common thought accompanying such attacks. Worry about completely losing control may also accompany a panic attack. Although panic attacks usually last only minutes, they cause considerable distress when they occur. In addition, it is common for the person to develop an anticipatory fear of helplessness that interferes with going into public places away from home or makes the person reluctant to be alone.

Shame. Much has been written about the relationship between shame and addiction. Regardless of the specific addiction, shameful feelings go hand in hand with addiction. Shame is an internal feeling of being inadequate, weak, or defective. It implies that something is wrong with us as people rather than with how we behave. Shame makes you feel like you are a bad person. It is a major factor in low self-esteem, which is often associated with addiction. In some cases, shame contributes to self-hatred, a feeling of really despising yourself. Rather than face shame, people may decide to go back to their addictions as one way of temporarily blotting out the feelings.

POSITIVE EMOTIONAL STATES

Small but significant numbers of addicts are more prone to relapse when they experience positive emotional states. These positive states may originate from interactions with other people or from within themselves. Research by doctors Cummings, Gordon, and Marlatt found that about eleven percent of relapses were attributed to positive emotions by a cross section of alcoholics, drug addicts, addicted smokers, compulsive gamblers, and overeaters. This relapse factor was found to be higher among overeaters, heroin addicts, and smokers.

Feeling good may contribute to relapse in a number of ways. It can make you less vigilant about your recovery by giving you a false sense of security and control. Or you may tell yourself that since you feel so good, you deserve a reward—however, it just so happens that the reward is using the addictive substance or engaging in the addictive behavior. In some cases, feeling good may be an early warning sign of an impending manic episode among people with bipolar illness. Consider the case of

Michael, a sales executive with both a bipolar illness (manic depression) and a compulsive sexual disorder.

"Before I went into a manic episode, subtle changes happened. I would start feeling real good, like things were going great. It seemed like my life was finally in order. I then made a lot of phone calls to family members, business associates, and friends to catch up on things. I was feeling so good and bursting with energy, I soon talked myself into calling old lovers. First it was a drink and dinner with one. Then another. Then another. Quickly, it got out of hand. I was seeing four or five different women at a time. Sometimes, two in one night! My compulsive sexual behavior started back again."

URGES, CRAVINGS, AND DESIRES

All addicts in recovery will at one time or another feel an urge to engage in the addictive behavior again. Although urges or desires can be experienced at any point in recovery, they tend to be most common in the early months or first year or so. The nature of addiction is such that these can occur naturally, without anything to trigger them. In other words, being a drug addict makes you susceptible to wanting or craving drugs. Or being a sex addict makes you susceptible to wanting or craving whatever sexual behaviors are part of your addiction.

However, in most instances you can trace these urges, cravings, or desires to internal or external stimuli. Internal feelings of discomfort may lead to increased desires or urges to engage in your addictive habit or behavior. Kathy is a case in point. When she feels upset and despondent, she finds that there are several ways she can deal with this discomfort. One way is to fill herself with food. Kathy often uses overeating binges in an attempt to make herself feel better. And, it works . . . for awhile.

External stimuli can trigger cravings or desires as well. Such stimuli are the things, people, places, activities, or experiences that are associated with addiction. These associations can be either positive or negative and they can vary in their strength. Although each person has his or her own unique set of stimuli that may trigger a strong desire or craving, some are fairly common among the different addictions. For example, one study of alcoholics beginning recovery found a significant increase in cravings to drink when they held liquor in their hands. Another study of heroin addicts recently detoxified from drugs found similar increased cravings in response to viewing a videotape that showed needles, drugs, and other paraphernalia associated with drug use.

The following list gives some associations with addictions that were related by a cross section of people.

- *Alcoholism.* David felt a desire to drink as he prepared for his company's Fourth of July picnic. That year's picnic was his first time to go as a sober man intending to stay sober. All of his recollections of the picnic were of drinking and getting drunk. Stimuli increasing the desire to drink commonly reported by alcoholics include seeing advertisements for liquor, smelling or seeing an alcoholic beverage, or driving past old hangouts where they used to drink.

- *Drugs.* Kay, a physician in an emergency room, experienced a mild craving for drugs after sorting through a patient's medication bottles during an evaluation. The patient had several bottles of pills including Percodan, Kay's drug of choice during her addiction. Smelling marijuana burning, getting a flu shot with a needle, seeing baby powder spilled over a coffee table (a reminder of cocaine), seeing pills or a rock of crack, or hearing rock and roll music (a reminder of getting high) are some stimuli that trigger cravings for drug addicts. One heroin addict stated, "Anytime I get sick and nauseous and feel like throwing up, I get an itch for dope. It reminds me of shooting up."

- *Overeating.* The smell of fresh bread and pastries hit Howard hard when he stopped to pick up a birthday cake for his secretary. He bought an extra half dozen of his favorite pastries and left them in his car so he could have a little snack that night. Later that day at work, he came to his senses and removed the pastries from his car to give them to a colleague. Since compulsive overeaters cannot stop eating completely, stimuli for food are everywhere; however, certain stimuli can trigger a craving for food, particularly food that may be off limits as part of their recovery.

- *Sex.* Kathy watched a movie in which there were several hot and heavy love scenes. It aroused her sexual desires and significantly increased her thoughts of sex. Bruce, whose sexual addiction included initiating contact with young children, felt a sudden desire after watching a school bus unload children at school.

- *Gambling.* David, who had bet heavily on just about anything imaginable, was cleaning his dresser when he found an old score card from a golf game on which he had won a large amount of money. He began reminiscing about the game, which in turn triggered a desire for some gambling action.

OBSESSIONS AND FAULTY THINKING

Obsessions are recurrent ideas, thoughts, images, or impulses that invade your consciousness. You usually do not feel like you have much control over these things. They may be a fairly constant preoccupation with the object of your addiction (alcohol, drugs, sex, food, gambling), or they may pop in and out of your consciousness at various times. Regardless of your pattern of obsessions, the result is often the same—feeling overwhelmed, uncomfortable, and controlled. Obsessions go hand in hand with addiction and for some people are a tremendous source of torment because they can be hard to get rid of.

Faulty thinking, referred to as "stinking" thinking in self-help programs, means beliefs that are not accurate or specific thoughts that may support the addiction. Faulty beliefs or negative thoughts support addiction by letting you talk yourself into engaging in the addictive habit again. Some examples of these ideas include:

I'm a bad person, so why not use drugs [eat, gamble, have sex]?

I'm worthless.

Gambling [drugs, alcohol, sex, food] is the only thing that gives me a lift and makes me feel good.

Sex [drugs, alcohol, gambling, food] is the only thing that will meet my needs.

I can't have fun unless I get some sex [drugs, alcohol, gambling, food].

Relapse can't happen to me.

I'm in control now. I'll never go back to where I was before.

Recovery is such a drag. It's going so slow and ain't what it's cracked up to be.

PAINFUL MEMORIES

Many addicted individuals report very painful memories of events and situations experienced during their lives. While some of these memories have their roots in the early years of their lives, others relate to things that happened during adulthood. Hal, a Vietnam combat veteran who was decorated for gallant action on the battlefield, was tormented for many years by memories of watching other soldiers die. "It was not just the fact that they got killed, but how they died. I watched one guy get his legs and an arm blown off and scream in agony before he died. One of my buddies bled all over me from wounds."

Addicts, particularly those born into troubled families, report many extremely upsetting experiences like violence, incest, rape, and emotional abuse. Larry, a sex addict, both of whose parents were alcoholics and abusive, recalls with great pain an episode that took place when he was about five or six years old. "Mom and Dad often were both drunk together. They would yell and scream at each other. I remember feeling real scared and losing control of my bowels, messing up my pants. Well, when my mother found out she got nasty. She even threatened to make me eat it if I ever went in my pants again." Larry was exposed to many years of cruel treatment by both of his parents. He often blotted out his rage by getting high or having sex. These were two ways of comforting himself.

As I mentioned before, painful memories of such experiences lead to a range of intense feelings. Anger, fear, anxiety, and depression are some of the more common feelings associated with such memories.

SOCIAL PRESSURES

Substances such as alcohol, drugs, or food, and opportunities for gambling and sex, are all around us. Every addict is confronted with a variety of direct and indirect social pressures that, if not handled properly, can contribute to a relapse to the addiction. One group of researchers found social pressures to be the second most common factor involved in relapses of alcoholics, smokers, heroin addicts, gamblers, and overeaters. About 20 percent of all the relapses among these different groups were associated with social pressure. Heroin addicts (36 percent) and smokers (32 percent) were the two groups at highest risk, and gamblers (5 percent) were at lowest risk of relapse following exposure to social pressures.

You may be directly offered alcohol, drugs, food, sex, or an opportunity to gamble. The other person may work quite hard at convincing you to use the addictive substance or engage in the addictive behavior: "C'mon, just one drink or bet." "This coke [pot, speed, acid] is great stuff." "It's only booze, not drugs, so it won't hurt you." "Try some of this delicious cake [pie, casserole]." "I've got some good inside information about the game [race, fight]."

The pressure also may be more subtle, or even indirect. Being around others or participating in events where there is an opportunity to engage in your addictive habit can create internal pressure. One gay sex addict reported, "Whenever I go to gay bars to socialize, I often relapse. Even when I have no intention of going home with someone, I usually end doing so. It's like my sexual appetite is reawakened once I'm there." A female sex addict explained, "I relapsed after visiting a friend who insisted that I had to see a new videotape with these gorgeous men in it. After reluctantly giving in, I was turned on from watching the tape. So I rented some on my way home and bought a couple of nude magazines. Using porno always leads me to compulsive masturbating. Then, I get compelled to seek out numerous sex partners. Imagine, all of this started as a result of visiting a friend whom I knew was into sex movies and magazines." Even though this woman's relapse process probably started before she went to her friend's house, once there she was subjected to pressures to view a tape. From then on, it was downhill for her.

SPECIAL EVENTS AND HOLIDAYS

Sometimes invitations to special social events—an office party, a dinner at a friend's or relative's, a wedding, a graduation, an athletic event, or other special celebration—can create pressures.

Pressures may come from others or from within, especially when you feel good or in a celebratory mood. Many ex-smokers, for example, report that cocktail parties pose a threat to them because drinking and smoking go hand in hand. One alcoholic man said that annual superbowl parties were a high risk for him, while an Irish alcoholic woman reported that St. Patrick's day festivities always made her feel more vulnerable to drinking.

Many special events and activities occur during holidays and pose a threat for some addicts, particularly alcoholics, drug addicts, and overeaters. Office parties, family dinners, and parties with friends happen with great frequency. Many overeaters have slipped back to old eating patterns during the Thanksgiving and Christmas holiday seasons. Gaining just a few pounds creates a serious crisis for many who feel bad about this.

For some, certain holidays, such as Christmas, are high-risk because they are associated with a lot of bad memories. Bad memories may trigger feelings such as sadness, depression, and anger. These feelings in turn can make you feel more susceptible to relapse.

By anticipating the social pressures likely to arise in your life, the high-risk special events or holidays, and the thoughts and feelings they will trigger, and by planning how you can handle these, you will be better able to protect your recovery. You are less likely to be taken by surprise if you plan ahead.

NEGATIVE SOCIAL NETWORKS

The term social network refers to the people in your life with whom you are socially or emotionally involved. Such people are the family members and friends with whom you spend time and share similar interests or activities. They often have influence on the things you do, how you spend your time, and whether or not your needs are satisfied. They also influence your emotions and can have a role in supporting or helping your recovery. Research has shown, for example, that alcoholics and drug addicts with social and family stability have fewer problems in recovery than others. This research has also shown that relationships with other alcoholics or drug addicts can play a role in sabotaging your recovery, particularly when such people exert a negative influence on you. For example, if you are married and your spouse abuses drugs, it will be harder for you to live with this person and maintain your recovery. By the same token, if most or all of your friends get high and/or are addicted to alcohol or other drugs, and you continue actively socializing with them, your risk of relapse increases. This is why Alcoholics Anonymous and Narcotics Anonymous advise recovering addicts to try to avoid "people, places and things" associated with using substances.

Relationships with others who share your addictive habits or behaviors can increase your chances of relapse. Rose's inner group of friends shares her strong interest in cooking. They constantly exchange recipes, shop together, cook for each other, and talk for hours about recipes, food they have eaten, or restaurants they have gone to. Food and eating are the topics most talked about in this group. The vast majority of their social activities revolve around eating experiences. In fact, Rose's favorite pastime was preparing elaborate meals for friends. After she entered a recovery program for compulsive overeaters, Rose became aware that, without intending to, these good friends exerted a negative influence on her. Simply being invited to participate in social activities with them became quite difficult for her. Their interest in food and eating continued, while she was trying to direct her interests and activities elsewhere. Since she genuinely enjoyed their company, it became an increasingly difficult issue for her to face in her recovery.

Don, who loved gambling, went through a similar experience after he stopped his compulsive gambling. Like Rose, most of his friends shared his passion for gambling. Whenever he saw any of them, they talked continuously about lotteries, poker games, sports events, and a lot of other gambling activities. The fact that Don had stopped gambling was inconsequential to them. The old excitement associated with figuring out point spreads and arguing over why teams did or did not beat the spread came back when Don saw his gambling buddies. He quickly discovered that staying clean from gambling was not compatible with socializing with these people. This realization was very difficult for him to face because he had known these friends for a long time.

CONFLICTS IN RELATIONSHIPS

Problems or serious conflicts in relationships with family, friends, or others may trigger a relapse, particularly when negative feelings or irrational thoughts are experienced. "My wife really got on my nerves," said Paul, a recovering alcoholic. "We were arguing about one of our sons, and she accused me of taking sides with him. Well, things started getting out of control and my wife cussed me out. So I thought, 'The hell with this. I don't have to take this crap from her.' Rather than stay and deal with her head on, I stormed out of the house. I kept thinking that I'll show her. Got my revenge by getting half looped." Paul knew, however, that getting revenge on his wife by drinking was irrational and immature. He admitted he always had trouble settling arguments with her and hated it when she was right. He just could not stand conflict, especially if he was wrong about something. A quick escape to drinking only made matters worse in the long run.

Giving up an addiction may change things in your family. Odd as it may sound, stopping your addictive habit is likely to create a certain amount of stress and discomfort for your family. They have to get used to the new you and it is not always easy to do this. Recovery automatically brings about some conflict, which others may act out either consciously or unconsciously. Some addicts feel that certain family members prefer them to be involved in their addictive habit. This can happen without anything explicitly being said about it.

Conflict arises as well from the negative effects addiction has on the family. Much pain and suffering is inflicted on the family in the course of addiction. Resentment, anger, and other feelings may stay with family members for a long time, even after you have been in recovery from your addiction for some time. Remember, just because you stop your addiction does not ensure your family will embrace you with open arms. If your family was deeply hurt by your addiction and you never made amends to them, the chances of conflict are even greater.

Difficulties with friends, coworkers, or others are likely to arise as well. If you are not prepared to handle these conflicts, you can make yourself vulnerable to relapse. Later chapters discuss recovery issues pertinent to your family and relationships in greater detail.

IMPULSIVENESS

"Act before you think" is the motto of the impulsive person. Although with most relapses there tends to be at least some period of buildup, sometimes relapses happen impulsively. You may decide on the spur of the moment to engage in your addiction, often without regard to any potential negative consequences. You can act impulsively in response to social pressures, other environmental cues, internal pressures, or internal discomfort. Impulsive actions such as abruptly stopping therapy or participation in self-help programs can end in relapse as well.

Rash or hasty decisions made impulsively, even if they seem totally unrelated to your addiction, can eventually have an impact on relapse. Making significant decisions in your life without thinking them through can backfire. For example, Milt was doing very well in his recovery from addictive gambling. Slowly, he began to put his life and family back together. For the first time in years, he built a certain amount of routine into his life that provided him and his family with a degree of predictability that had been lacking for years. Rather hastily, he accepted a job offer with another company. Although he got a substantial raise in salary, his benefits were not as good, the company was not on as firm ground as his previous employer, and the job required him to move his family to another town. His wife and daughters were against the move and got angry with him. Several months after the job change, he realized what a bad mistake he had made. Milt was absolutely miserable. He eventually got so disgusted with himself that he rationalized that gambling would be the only way to put some pleasure and excitement back into his wretched life.

Although anyone may act impulsively at one time or another, some addicts tend to have an impulsive personality trait. Such people frequently act without thinking, or without considering the meaning of their behavior. Their impulsive behavior is seldom just one isolated incident. Instead, they make series of impulsive actions stemming from this personality trait. "I want what I want when I want it" is how one gambler put it when discussing his impulsiveness.

MULTIPLE ADDICTIONS

Many people have more than one addiction. It is not unusual for addictions to become linked, so that relapse to one can cause relapse to another. When a chemically dependent addict relapses to compulsive gambling or compulsive sexual behavior, one way to manage the feelings of guilt and shame that accompany the relapse is to drink alcohol or get high on other drugs. On the other hand, when an alcoholic or drug addict relapses to chemical use, his or her defenses may lower as judgment becomes more and more impaired. Under the influence of the chemical, the addict gives in to the wish to engage in the other addictive habit. A vicious cycle often ensues, leading to feelings of hopelessness and despair.

USING ALCOHOL OR DRUGS

People who are not addicted to alcohol or other drugs but who have other types of addictions often put themselves at risk of relapse simply by drinking alcohol or ingesting drugs. Research on ex-smokers has shown, for example, that after drinking alcohol a person is more likely to relapse to cigarette smoking.

Even in low or moderate doses, chemical substances such as alcohol and drugs lower inhibitions and affect judgment. A result can be a return to an addictive habit. "It was easier to talk myself into having a good time when I had a few drinks in me," said Nancy, a recovering sex addict. "A good time to me meant picking up guys and having wild sex. Guys I just met, whose only appeal to me was as a sex partner. Anytime I go to a party, if I don't limit myself to two drinks, my chances of relapsing to one of my sexual addictive behaviors increases significantly." Howard, a recovering compulsive eater, said, "Whenever I got buzzed up on pot, my diet went out the window. I'd binge on all kinds of junk food because I had such strong urges to pig out. I don't know, sometimes I wonder whether I used pot as a way of giving myself permission to binge. Staying in control was really hard for me."

MAJOR CHANGES AND STRESSES

Everyone is subject to major stresses or changes in life at one time or another. These may be unexpected or expected. Such events can be negative, such as losing your job or your partner; they can be positive, such as having a child, buying a house, moving to a new city, getting a promotion, or inheriting or winning a large sum of money. Change causes stress, and usually the greater the change, the more stress you feel.

Too much stress sometimes causes a person to backslide and rely on old coping mechanisms. For many, addictive substances or behaviors function as methods of stress reduction. An addiction is something that actually may seem to help in reducing stress, at least temporarily. Blair, a compulsive gambler, tells how he almost relapsed after he and his wife had their first child, and he had difficulty adjusting to this major life change. "After the initial excitement of being a father wore off, I suddenly realized how much work a new baby was. And, to top things off, my wife gave most of her time and energy to our baby daughter. Gradually, I found myself getting jealous. I was stressed out to the max because the baby was so much work and we were having a hard time meeting our bills since my wife quit her job. I won't lie to you. There were more than a few times when I thought to myself, 'The hell with this, I deserve a break' and thought of ways to sneak to the track. The idea of a few bets and spending time at the track was quite appealing. I'd be able to relax. Fortunately, I caught myself before I relapsed. I had to change some of my expectations about having a family. It helped a lot to talk to other fathers. Basically I found out that most people go through a major adjustment when they have their first child. Free time dwindles and money becomes tight, but most people survive it. So I made up my mind that I would do the best job I could with our baby and not be so jealous of getting less attention from my wife."

PHYSICAL PAIN OR MEDICAL PROBLEMS

Alcoholics and drug addicts sometimes relapse after experiencing physical pain or medical problems. Sometimes this happens when alcohol or other drugs are used to self-medicate pain; at other times it happens when certain types of medications are prescribed for dental, medical, or psychiatric problems. Pain medications and tranquilizers are used frequently for a variety of problems. A chemically dependent person's body cannot really tell the difference between a substance used to get high and one used for treatment of a problem. What happens for some is that even small dosages of medications trigger the addictive urge. I know of addicts who relapsed after taking a pain medicine following dental surgery.

PSYCHIATRIC ILLNESS

It is not uncommon to have a psychiatric illness in addition to an addiction. Some illnesses can create a lot of personal distress or suffering. Don, a recovering alcoholic, discovered long after getting sober that he had severe feelings of anxiety. "My nerves got so bad," he said, "that I thought I was going crazy or something. I tried so hard to make these feelings go away. But, it was just easier to drink. A few drinks would calm me down considerably." Don's problem was, however, that after a few drinks he had a few more. Then a few more. And then, he got drunk. This led to a vicious cycle in which he returned to active alcoholism. It was not until he finally got the right kind of treatment for his psychiatric illness that he was able to remain sober for any length of time.

A psychiatric illness can contribute to relapse in other ways. It can interfere with your judgment so that you make poor decisions and go back to your addictive habit. Do you remember the case discussed previously, in which the man with a bipolar disorder (an illness with mood swings from depression to euphoria) went back to compulsive sexual behavior? His relapse happened after his mood became elevated, his thoughts altered, and his behaviors changed. He called several of his ex-lovers and made arrangements to get together with them. It was not long before he was seeing five different women, sometimes two in the same day.

Your psychiatric illness also can affect your motivation or ability to work at your recovery plan. Connie worked hard at her recovery, but after about two years of success, she had a very serious episode of depression. Connie tried everything she could think of to fight off her depression, but it lingered on. As her energy declined and her interest in Alcoholics Anonymous waned, she cut down on and then stopped attending meetings. She simply quit caring because she felt so depressed. Connie ended up relapsing to alcohol use because she saw it as the one way she knew to at least temporarily blot out her psychological pain.

PROBLEMS WITH A RECOVERY PLAN

Problems with your recovery plan can also lead to relapse. Such problems come from two sources: you, and others you work with in therapy or recovery. If you are lazy and do not make much of an effort to change, or you try to take the "easy" road to recovery, or approach it halfheartedly, your chances of relapse increase. Or if you avoid working on important personal recovery issues, they can come back to haunt you. Jeanne's case is an example of this. "I never thought much about the need to make amends to anyone," she said. "It just never dawned on me that my overeating behavior had much of an effect on anybody but me. Yeah, I knew my husband was upset with me, but I had no idea how mad he really was. Anyways, what happened was that he blew up one day and threw all kinds of stuff up in my face. I felt guilty as hell, and really low. It really deflated me. I kinda gave up and went right on a binge. It really wasn't his fault as much as it was mine for not paying attention to the need to make amends. Guess it goes to show you how everybody gets affected by what you do."

On the other hand, counselors, sponsors, or even friends in self-help recovery programs can play a role in your relapse. They can give you poor advice or try to get you to move too quickly in your recovery. Or, as in the case of some professionals, they can misjudge you entirely and not notice that you have a psychiatric illness that may require additional treatment. "Wait until you stop your addiction for a while and your symptoms will go away" is the message given. Although this is true in some cases, in many other cases it is not, because a real psychiatric illness exists.

PROBLEMS WITH ATTITUDES
OR EXPECTATIONS

When first starting a recovery program, it is not unusual to be flooded with negative attitudes toward recovery or even toward people trying to help you. Such attitudes can lead to giving up and saying, "The hell with it! Why bother?" The real challenge of recovery is sticking with your program when you do not want to, when you do not care, when your attitude is very negative. As one compulsive gambler said, "Anyone can stay away from gambling when he wants to. It's really when you don't give a damn and want to gamble real bad that you are more likely to do it. Thing is, your attitude can change in a minute. One day you got it all under control and love recovery. Then zap, the next day you say the hell with it and wanna go to the track. Tell you this, the shit's confusing to me."

Sometimes you simply get tired of having to work at a recovery plan. It seems easier to give in. After doing well on a diet and a recovery program for compulsive overeating, Walt said, "I got tired of it. Tired of planning meals. Tired of OA meetings. Tired of thinking about recovery. I just had it up to here! So I went out and bought some stuff at a bakery. I treated myself. Now my problem was, I wouldn't have just one dessert, you know. Not me. Had to be the whole bag. Losing my interest definitely made me relapse."

Unrealistic or overly high expectations can also lead to relapse. You can set yourself up by placing your expectations of yourself or your recovery so high that it is impossible to reach them. Then, when you do not meet these expectations, you feel very bad and deal with your feelings by going back to your addictive substance or behavior. This is yet another example of the vicious cycle returning.

TESTING CONTROL

Some people relapse after putting themselves in situations in which they test themselves to see if they are strong enough to face their addiction and "not give in." Although there may be times when this behavior is reasonable, in the early phases of recovery people often purposely put themselves in situations in which they are tempted to engage in their addictive behavior. This may be an unconscious desire to return to the addictive habit or it may be a test of will to prove to themselves that they are strong.

LIFESTYLE IMBALANCE

Relapse sometimes stems from an accumulation of things, or from a way of living, rather than from one or more specific events or situations. If your lifestyle is not balanced, returning to your addiction may be quite attractive. This is especially true if your addiction was your primary source of pleasure.

A lifestyle is reasonably balanced when there are not too many "shoulds" or "obligations" at the expense of "wants" or "satisfactions." Modern life is filled with many responsibilities and obligations for most people; however, if you do not pay attention to your needs and fail to get things you need to bring you pleasure or satisfaction, you are likely to feel frustrated. If enough frustration builds up, it is easy to justify going back to your addictive substance or behavior.

Setting Priorities and Making an Action Plan

PRIORITIZING HIGH-RISK SITUATIONS

You cannot deal with all of your high-risk factors at once; such an attempt would be too overwhelming and could lead to giving up. To avoid this, try to put these high-risk factors in some order. Which one should you work on first? Which should you work on next? At times you may be dealing with more than one factor at once. For example, Joyce often binged on food when she got upset and angry at her husband. "This was my way of getting back at him. It seemed like a good reason to give in to my compulsion to eat." Joyce also set herself up to relapse by constantly planning elaborate dinner parties in which she would cook everything from scratch, from hors d'oeuvres to dessert. And, although she ate modestly during the actual dinner party, when people left and she cleaned up, she "attacked the leftovers." Joyce had to work on her attitudes and behaviors related to angry feelings and also those related to entertaining.

DEVELOPING AN ACTION PLAN

"Talk is cheap," said an alcoholic the other day. "You can be educated as hell about all this relapse stuff, but the bottom line is you gotta change!" What this man was saying is that you have to put your knowledge of yourself and your high-risk situations to work. Make an action plan. An action plan is simply a list of the things you will do to deal with your various high-risk factors. Actions may involve work on changing your attitudes, how you think, how you behave, or how you cope with things.

Your action plan should be as concrete as possible. For example, rather than saying, "I will talk to someone when I feel a compulsion to gamble," you should say, "I will talk to Roberta, my Gamblers Anonymous sponsor, or I will call Jan, my friend in GA and ask if I can come over to her house and talk when I feel overwhelmed by a compulsion to gamble." Your action plan should be something you can do now!

Action plans with multiple options are best. In this way, if one plan does not work, you can try another one. Many find it helpful to put their action plans in writing. This paper serves as a reminder, especially in times of stress.

Take two or three of your high-risk situations and practice developing a written action plan. Try to list at least five coping strategies for each relapse risk factor. Then, share this plan with someone you trust who understands addiction.

PRACTICING YOUR ACTION PLAN

When possible, practice your action plan before you actually try it in a real situation. Howard, who was recovering from compulsive overeating, spent a few minutes in front of the mirror each day imagining that he was being offered one of the food items he was trying to avoid. He practiced out loud refusing the offer of food. Ray, recovering from compulsive sexual behavior, practiced changing his thoughts about sex. For example, he allowed typical thoughts about sex with women to enter his mind, thoughts like "Just one more woman wouldn't hurt." He practiced making counterstatements such as, "No, no, no. One more woman would hurt. I won't allow myself to give in to my impulses. I have too much to gain by avoiding sexual entanglements."

IMPLEMENTING YOUR ACTION PLAN

"Just do it," as the commercial says! Put your plan of action to work. Do not be afraid of making mistakes. Mistakes are to be expected, especially at first. You can modify your plan as needed since recovery is an ongoing process, not something you do once and get over with.

Recovery is not an intellectual exercise; it is an active change of your attitudes and behaviors. As Alcoholics Anonymous says, "Walk the walk, don't just talk the talk." This simply means do what you say you need to do, do not just talk about it.

Many changes involve modifying both your attitudes and your behaviors. Sometimes, though, you have to change your behavior before your attitude changes. For example, Frank reluctantly went to Narcotics Anonymous meetings on the advice of his doctor. At first, he did not think it would help him withstand his strong desire to use cocaine. Even though he originally had a negative attitude toward Narcotics Anonymous, in time Frank found that its meetings helped him.

5

Dealing with Emotions

Your emotions or feelings have a great impact on your behavior. How you cope with your feelings—positive or negative ones—affects your recovery as well as your happiness in life. A major thrust of recovery from an addiction is handling your emotions in constructive and healthy ways. Learning this can help reduce the chances of relapsing and help you feel better about yourself and your life. Coping with your feelings in a healthy manner will also affect your relationships, as well as your physical and mental health.

For instance, while John was active in his addiction he swallowed his angry feelings and pretended that everything was always fine. He could not tell others, including his wife, when he was angry at them. After enough anger had built up, John would get drunk and then let it all out. The problem was that he said and did things to hurt others, which created serious problems in his relationships. John would then feel guilty about his behaviors. When John got sober, he had to learn to recognize and deal with his anger so that his recovery was not at risk. John says that since he learned when it is appropriate to express his anger and how to express it, he gets along better with people and hardly ever has the bad headaches he used to. John also has learned how to change his angry thoughts and talk himself out of his anger when it does not seem justified by the situation.

In the previous chapter, "High-Risk Relapse Factors," negative and positive emotions associated with relapse were discussed. In this chapter, the focus will be on ways in which you can learn new coping mechanisms to handle your feelings. Some of the more common emotional states reported by addicted individuals—anger, boredom, guilt, and so on—are discussed as well, so that you will have some ideas on how to deal with these particular emotional states.

Following are some steps you can take to help you deal with emotions. These steps can help you regardless of the particular emotion. Use the ones that make the most sense to you. Try not to feel that you have to rigidly adhere to all of these steps or even always use them. Sometimes you have to accept your feelings and wait until they change; you do not have to take any particular action.

Suggested Steps for Understanding and Handling Feelings

Step 1. Recognize and label your feelings.

Step 2. Be aware of how your feelings show in body language, physical symptoms, thoughts, and behaviors.

Step 3. Look for the causes of uncomfortable feelings (events, situations, perceptions, and attributions).

Step 4. Evaluate the effects of your emotions on yourself and other people.

Step 5. Learn new coping strategies to help you deal with emotions.

Step 6. Rehearse new coping strategies.

Step 7. Put your new coping strategies into action.

Step 8. Change your strategies as needed, based on an evaluation of whether or not they were effective.

RECOGNIZE YOUR FEELINGS

Coping with emotions begins with awareness of what you are feeling. As simple as this sounds, many people have trouble knowing what they feel. Many mislabel what they are feeling. For example, when you say to yourself, "I'm feeling upset," what do you really mean? Are you really saying you feel angry, disappointed, depressed, or ashamed?

When you first stop your addictive habit it is common to be flooded with many feelings that seem rather foreign. Often you feel uncomfortable with these emotions, especially if your addiction covered them up. Being aware of when you feel happy, sad, angry, bored, guilty, and so on is a good way to begin the process of handling emotions in a constructive way. Try not to deny or minimize your true emotions.

Following are some questions for you to reflect on to raise your self-awareness of your feelings.

Do you seem to experience certain feelings more than others? If yes, which ones?

Do you tend to avoid certain feelings or find them very uncomfortable? If yes, which ones?

Is there a balance between experiences of negative and positive emotions in your life? If not, why not?

Is there a balance between expressing positive and negative feelings? If not, why not?

Are you mainly aware of, or more apt to express, your negative feelings? If so, why?

Which feelings make you feel most vulnerable to relapsing to your addiction?

What you allow yourself to feel and how you deal with your feelings are influenced by your attitudes and beliefs. In thinking about your emotional life, try to see if there are any patterns. For example, while evaluating himself, Steve found that it was much easier for him to express negative feelings towards others. No one walked on Steve or upset him without hearing about it. Unfortunately, Steve had immense difficulty in sharing positive feelings. When he cared about or loved someone, he seldom if ever expressed it. He operated under the belief that "sharing love and affection make you emotionally vulnerable" and that "to be in control, don't tell people you care about them." Steve's problem was that his relationships with women usually ended in disaster because his tendency to quickly and frequently express criticism, anger, or disappointment was not balanced by expressions of love or tenderness. As a result, he pushed women away by belittling them all the time.

BE AWARE OF HOW YOUR FEELINGS SHOW

Your emotions show in your gestures, thoughts, and behaviors. Depending on the specific feeling, you may experience physical signs, such as tenseness in your stomach, sweaty palms, headaches, moving much more slowly than normal, or speaking more quickly than normal. Psychological signs may include giving negative messages to yourself ("I'm a failure," or "I can't handle this situation or person"), revenge fantasies ("I'll get even"), or increased thoughts about your addictive substance or behavior ("A few bets/drugs/alcohol/food/sex are needed to make me feel better"). Behavioral signs show in how you act. For example, when angry, some people lash out at others, some withdraw and avoid other people, and some are passive-aggressive (for example, they "forget" a spouse's birthday or are late for a dinner that their spouse put effort into preparing). When bored, some people look for risky activities to get involved in, others escape into excessive sleeping or television watching, and some go on shopping sprees and spend money. Although many common physical, psychological, and behavioral signs exist, each person has very personal ones.

Self-Awareness Task 5–1: *Recognizing Signs of Feelings*

Identify two feelings that are difficult for you to deal with. For each of these feelings, identify how they show in:

your body (physical signs)

your internal messages, or what you think or say to yourself (psychological signs)

your actions or behaviors (behavioral signs)

With practice and continued vigilance, you may learn to interpret some of these signs so that you more easily recognize the feeling they reflect. For example, Bert identified tightness in his stomach, excessive worrying, and fidgeting as signs of feeling anxious. Once he knew this, Bert was able to look at where his anxiety was coming from and decide what he could do to cope with it.

Before he reached this understanding, he did not connect these signs with his anxious feelings.

LOOK FOR THE CAUSES OF UNCOMFORTABLE FEELINGS

When you experience an emotion that is uncomfortable and causes you problems or distress, try to find out where it is coming from. Is it connected to some external event, situation, or encounter with someone? Or is it mainly internal from your thoughts or beliefs?

Your attitudes and beliefs can play a role in your emotions. For example, if you grew up in a family where an angry parent displayed violence, you may have learned to associate the two. In this case, anger equals violence in your view. If you connect the two and are afraid of becoming violent, you may then deny angry feelings or do everything in your power to avoid expressing them. A result is that your anger builds up.

An interesting distinction to make is whether or not a feeling represents a state or a trait. Consider two people who are depressed. One feels depressed because of a major disappointment, but he gets used to the disappointment and learns to deal with it. Soon, he no longer feels depressed. His state of depression leaves. Another person feels depressed most of the time. Nothing has to happen to trigger this feeling of depression. He is considered by many friends and family members to be a depressed person. His depression is less of an emotional state, and more of a trait. It is part of his emotional makeup or personality style. This person is likely to think in depressed ways.

Avoid blaming others for how you feel. Although others' behavior can affect your emotions, ultimately you must own up to them because you decide what you will feel.

Self-Awareness Task 5–2: *Finding the Causes of Uncomfortable Feelings*

Reflect on one or two feelings that you have difficulty dealing with.

What are the causes of these feelings?

What are the external sources (outside of you)?

What are the internal sources (inside you)?

EVALUATE THE EFFECTS OF YOUR EMOTIONS

Evaluating your emotions involves taking a close look at how your feelings and how you cope with them affect you and other people in your life. Usually there will be a combination of positive and negative effects. When you evaluate how a given feeling affects you, think in terms of your overall physical and mental health. You can consider how your feelings affect your ability to meet your needs in life as well as how your relationships with others are affected. For example, if you are constantly angry, bored, or depressed, others close to you are likely to be affected in one way or another. They may feel like they are walking on eggshells and try very hard to not do anything that they think will upset you. Or they may feel responsible for how you feel or for making you feel better.

Self-Awareness Task 5–3: *Evaluating Your Emotions*

One way to raise your awareness of the effects of your emotions and of your coping behavior is to choose two specific feelings that you wish to improve your ability to cope with. How do these feelings and the way you handle them affect

your physical health?

your mental health?

your spiritual health?

how you behave toward other people?

how other people relate to you?

your family life?

your ability to work?

your self-esteem?

Liz, a compulsive overeater, wants to improve her ability to deal with loving feelings. She habitually keeps these feelings to herself. The result is that Liz berates herself, questions her capacity to maintain a mutually satisfying relationship with a man, and cannot get close to others. Although holding back these feelings is safe and prevents her from getting hurt, it also prevents her from establishing emotionally satisfying relationships.

When Liz realizes that she feels strong love for a man, she usually does something to sabotage the relationship. She is very unhappy and lonely as a result. Liz often indulges in eating binges after intense feelings of loneliness. She is caught in a vicious cycle. Liz must recognize the impact of her feelings on her life before she will be able to get a handle on how to change it.

LEARN NEW COPING STRATEGIES

You have to figure out different ways of dealing with your emotions if the old ways cause distress or problems in your life or if they make you vulnerable to returning to your addictive habit. No single approach works for all people, so it is best to find the ways that work for you. Because one way of coping with an emotional state can be successful in one instance but not in another, it is helpful to have several different coping strategies. For example, when you feel very bored and restless, you may get over this feeling by keeping busy with a hobby or work activity at home. However, sometimes this coping strategy may not work. Then, perhaps, you need to get out of your home and go somewhere else, or perhaps get together and socialize with family or friends. Or you may simply weather the storm and tell yourself that your boredom is temporary and will pass. The more coping strategies you have, the better off you are. Coping strategies fall into one of the several general types listed below:

- *Cognitive.* This term refers to changing your beliefs or how you think about your feelings or situation. For example, you may have to change your belief "If I'm angry I have to hurt other people" to "I can feel angry at others and still get along with them. I don't have to hurt them physically or emotionally just because I feel angry at them." Or an alcoholic who gets angry at her husband and thinks "I'll get even with him by getting drunk" may have to change this to "I'm so upset I feel like getting drunk. But that won't do anything but make the situation worse. I guess I'll take a walk and cool off and think about what I'm going to do to get through to my stubborn husband."
- *Behavioral.* This term refers to redirecting your activity and doing something different. For example, rather than staying

home by yourself and feeling increasingly lonely, you can call a friend and invite him or her to go to a movie or to some other activity. Or you may call family or friends and talk on the telephone. Frank, a recovering sex addict, was prone to relapse when he sat at home by himself on Saturday nights. This was the evening he associated with picking up multiple sex partners or spending hours calling sex hot lines. In the early months of his recovery Frank found it helpful to have plans for each Saturday evening that got him out of his apartment and kept him from being alone. Slowly, he was able to break the association between Saturday evening and sex with strangers. Frank eventually reached the point where he could stay home alone and not call the sex hot lines.

- *Expressive.* This term refers to expressing your feelings directly to those about whom you feel them or talking about your feelings with another person whom you trust. For example, you may tell your son or daughter, "I am disappointed that you did so poorly in school and didn't listen to your mother and me." Or you may say to your spouse, "Sometimes I get so furious with my boss I'd like to give him a piece of my mind." Putting your feelings into words often helps to reduce their intensity. A note of caution is in order, however. I do not advocate the free expression of all of your feelings. It is not always appropriate to express what you are feeling. Sometimes it is in your best interests, or the best interests of others, not to express your feelings directly.

- *Avoidance.* This term refers to avoiding people, places, and things that would put you at risk of relapse when you feel a particular emotion. If you are a compulsive gambler and feel bored, going to the race track, a gambling casino, or to a friend's where there is a poker game would not be wise. If you are a recovering drug addict, seeking out an old friend with whom you previously got high or going to a party where drugs are flowing freely would make little sense.

In your quest to develop new coping mechanisms, be realistic about what you can change, how quickly you can change, and how you can go about making the changes you want to make. Also keep in mind that there is a difference between short-term and long-term coping mechanisms. For example, in the case of Frank, the sex addict cited above, his short-term coping strategy was to keep busy outside of his apartment on Saturday evenings. This routine helped him control his impulses to pick up multiple sex partners or to spend hours talking on sex hot lines while he masturbated. For the long term, however, Frank had to learn to trust others and develop the capacity for a truly intimate relationship. This change brought him satisfaction and helped fill the emotional void that he previously had tried to fill temporarily with compulsive sexual activities such as masturbation, picking up strange women or prostitutes, and calling sex hot lines.

REHEARSE NEW COPING STRATEGIES

Practice, practice, practice! You will not necessarily change just because you have identified, or talked about, changing and learning new coping methods. In many instances you first have to practice what you are going to do. For example, perhaps you feel anxious about how to refuse offers from others to engage in your addictive habit, and you focus on two new coping strategies: (1) self-talk and (2) refusal skills. You may repeatedly practice telling yourself things such as "It's OK to feel anxious, I don't have to give in to my anxiety by getting back into my addiction." Or, "Once I get used to refusing, I'll feel less and less anxious. Things will feel better in time." Or you may imagine that others ask you to engage in your addictive habit and practice saying no out loud. After you have practiced by yourself, you may then practice your responses on another person (friend, family member, counselor, or sponsor). Then, when you are in the actual situation, you are likely to feel more confident about what you will say and how you will handle the situation. Rehearsing first can help you work on the rough spots, learn from your mistakes, raise your awareness of how you will think and feel in the situation when it happens in real life, and raise your confidence level by making you feel better prepared.

In his recovery from compulsive overeating, Howard had to deal with his anxiety about eating desserts. His love of desserts often led to relapsing and going on eating binges. Howard practiced thinking differently about desserts to help control his anxiety. He had originally believed that "a good dessert is essential to top off a good meal" and that "skipping dessert means punishing myself." Howard had to change these thoughts to "desserts really are good, but I'm working hard at cutting them out. Think of how much weight I can lose simply by not eating desserts." Howard also thought, "I can still enjoy a meal by eating moderately and skipping dessert. It's not punishing myself. It's being reasonable and following my recovery program." Practicing these thought changes helped him control and eventually reduce his anxious feelings. Because he frequently ate at restaurants with business clients, Howard also found it helpful to practice different ways of refusing desserts. He practiced responding with humor, which made him feel less self-conscious. Practicing ahead of time made him less anxious when Howard actually had to put this strategy to the test.

PUT YOUR NEW COPING STRATEGIES INTO ACTION

Do not forget the wonderful saying of the self-help programs: "Walk the walk, don't just talk the talk." Stated simply, this means that you need to translate your recovery plan into action. Do not just talk about changing or coping. Do it! You can come up with a long list of brilliant coping strategies to help deal with emotions or problems, but it means absolutely nothing if you are not actually able to use these strategies in your daily life. I have known many addicted people who relapsed because they did not utilize coping strategies. If you find yourself resisting the idea of using your new coping strategies, try to figure out why. Although it may seem easier to do things the old way, if you do not find new alternatives for coping with your feelings, you are more at risk of relapse.

CHANGE YOUR STRATEGIES AS NEEDED

Recovery and relapse prevention are ongoing processes. You may need to change your coping strategies as time goes on. What helped you at one time may no longer help you now. The idea of practicing and then using new coping responses is to find out what will work best for you. Use what works and get rid of the rest.

When you first try new ways of coping with your emotions, you can expect to feel uncomfortable, awkward, or even unsure of yourself. It takes time to develop confidence in your new coping skills. You need to use them and feel successful before your confidence level will rise. It a coping strategy does not work in a particular situation, do not assume it will not work in a similar situation in the future. On the other hand, however, if you try the same coping strategy many times, only to find it ineffective, then you should try different strategies. Try to do this without labeling yourself as a failure. Perhaps the particular unsuccessful coping strategy simply was not the right one for you.

Coping with High-Risk Emotions

In chapter 4, "High-Risk Relapse Factors," negative and positive emotions associated with relapse were discussed. In the remainder of this chapter, ways of dealing with some of the more common emotional states—anger, anxiety, boredom, depression, guilt, and shame—will be reviewed. The experiences of people recovering from addictions will be shared as a way to illustrate various coping mechanisms.

ANGER

Problems with anger can show in many different ways. Sometimes the problems are quite obvious, while at other times they are subtle or hidden. The case of John, which follows, shows how holding on to his anger played a role in his compulsive overeating and feelings of dissatisfaction.

"I don't want to hurt anyone's feelings. Most people consider me a pretty nice guy. I'm usually pretty friendly and helpful. The problem is, I'm too damn nice most of the time. I bend over backwards for people, especially if I think they are upset or mad at me. When they do something that really bugs me or hurts me, I never say anything. I just don't want to rock the boat, so I keep my anger to myself. It makes me feel dissatisfied with myself and my life. I've noticed that when I'm really steaming at somebody, I eat a lot. If I'm at work, I'll visit the snack bar and munch

on anything and everything. If I'm at home, I'll attack the refrigerator. Eating seems to calm me down, at least for a while."

Fortunately for John, he got a handle on how to deal with his angry feelings. It took him a long time, but he learned to accept his angry feelings as legitimate and rational. John learned that sometimes it was appropriate to let the other person know how he felt and he began to share his feelings with some people. He also had to challenge his distorted notions that "being angry means you don't like the other person" and "getting mad at somebody risks ruining the relationship." John changed these thoughts to "you can get mad at people you like—everybody does it" and "it's better for a relationship to be honest and say what you really feel instead of letting things build up." Addicted people seem especially prone to holding on to angry feelings for a long time and letting them build up. Or they act them out, often inappropriately, at the expense of others.

Judy's situation with anger is entirely different. She is an "angry person," who lashes out at anyone and everyone. Judy, a cocaine addict, is always getting into conflicts with others because of her style of dealing with her feelings.

"I was an angry SOB. For years, I was like a walking timebomb. Everything and everybody pissed me off. I could get mad at a four-year-old child in a grocery store as easy as getting mad at my boss. Seemed like I was always ready to jump on somebody. I could give quite a tongue-lashing, usually for stupid little things which really were no big deal. When I was high on drugs, I sometimes got physically violent. I'm not a very big woman but I've gone wild a couple times and broken more things than I care to remember.

"I can't tell you the number of problems I caused with people because of my short fuse. A lot of people avoided me. Even my friends got tired of my shenanigans. My first husband divorced me and several other men ditched me because of my temper.

"In recovery I learned that the problem was me, not other people. This was a very hard pill to swallow because at first I was convinced that the problem was everybody else and not me. After all, 'they' were pissing me off and causing me to get mad and act nasty!"

It would not have been appropriate for Judy simply to learn how to express her anger to others. In the vast majority of situations, Judy's anger was not justified. Her problem was much deeper and was related more to a character trait than to her way of coping with anger. Judy had to correct her distorted views of the world and herself. Slowly, she moved from blaming others for her problems and feelings to accepting that she was the problem. As her thinking changed, Judy learned to control her impulses and not lash out at others. She struggled, because it was not easy to think before acting and accepting personal responsibility for her feelings was new to her. Judy had been used to acting at once, without much thought; now her violent acting out has stopped completely. Judy still sometimes gets herself into trouble with her comments, but she admits that things are much improved compared to the past.

Learning new ways of expressing or reevaluating your anger will be uncomfortable at first. You may even surprise people in your life and make them also feel uncomfortable. If your spouse is used to you stuffing your anger, he or she may not know how to deal with you when you suddenly become direct with your feelings. Do not be surprised if some people prefer you the way you were before you changed.

You may find it helpful to complete an "anger check" at the end of each day. You simply ask yourself if you have any angry feelings that you have not dealt with, and then you look at where they are coming from and what you should do about them. The purpose of such an anger check is to prevent angry feelings from building up over time and to practice anger recognition on a regular basis. This exercise is particularly helpful if you are the type of person who ignores, denies, or stuffs angry feelings. If your anger arises from a character trait, an anger check can help you more clearly see patterns. You can use the check as a daily reminder that your anger usually is not justified and results more from your views of the world than from harm that other people actually do to you.

The list below presents some methods you can use to handle anger.

Decide first if your anger is really justified. Is it appropriate to the situation or the result of a character trait?

If you are an angry person—someone who seems to get angry too often or for no good reason—work on changing your character.

Talk directly to the person toward whom you feel angry.

Talk about your angry feelings with a friend, family member, counselor, or sponsor. Share your feelings at a self-help meeting. Many people "drop off" their resentments at twelve-step meetings.

Direct your angry feelings toward physical activities such as running or working around the house.

Change your thoughts and beliefs about angry feelings or how you should handle them.

Do not let your anger build up. Do an anger check each day to make sure you are not holding your feelings inside.

ANXIETY

Anxious feelings are common in recovery. When you give up an addictive habit, you are likely to feel anxious for a while. You may wonder if you can handle the demands of recovery and worry about whether or not you will relapse. Anxiety may stem from the typical challenges of recovery, such as how to handle a craving to indulge in your addictive substance or habit. A strong desire for cocaine will cause a drug addict to feel anxious. A strong desire for gambling will make a compulsive gambler experience anxiety. Increased fantasies and thoughts about sex can cause anxiety in a sex addict. Eating in moderation in front of other people can cause a compulsive overeater to feel anxious. Each addiction creates its own challenges for the person who attempts to recover from it.

You may feel anxious because you have to face the problems and consequences of your addiction. Perhaps your family was hurt deeply and you now have to face them. Or perhaps you suffered major losses because of your addiction and you now have to face them—for example, an important person ended the relationship with you, you lost your job, or you lost considerable money.

Facing life without the addictive crutch is certainly not easy. Even though your addiction caused you problems, it did help control your anxiety, at least temporarily. When you face life on its own terms, it is natural to feel anxious, especially if you had your addiction for many years. Perhaps you have to face the fact that you despise your job or that you and your spouse have very serious problems that may not be solvable. Facing these or similar issues is going to cause you to feel anxious. Being in recovery is like looking at life from a different point of view and anything new is likely to evoke anxious feelings. Change itself causes anxiety!

Your addiction gave one kind of structure to your life, and recovery disrupts this structure. You often experience feelings of anxiety when you look at yourself and your lifestyle and realize that you have to change many things. Where do you start? What will it be like? What will you be like as a recovering person? Can you succeed in your recovery? How will others respond to you? These are just a few questions you may ask yourself that can trigger anxious feelings.

In cases of alcoholism and drug addiction, anxiety can result from your body's adjustment to being without chemicals. Anxiety, depression, and cravings are just a few of the common symptoms of sobriety experienced by alcoholics and drug addicts, particularly in the first several months of recovery.

Excessive use of caffeine, tobacco, and food products such as sugar can also increase your anxiety level. Lifestyle factors such as a lack of exercise or recreation can indirectly contribute to your anxiety as well.

Persistent, unrealistic, or excessive dread or worry that cause significant problems in your life may be signs of an anxiety disorder. This state is much more serious than the feelings of anxiety discussed previously. There are several different types of anxiety disorders, any of which can interfere with your recovery from addiction. One type is panic disorder. A panic disorder involves several of the following symptoms: dizziness, faintness, or unsteadiness; shortness of breath or smothering sensations; heart palpitations; shaking and trembling; sweating; choking; nausea or upset stomach; a feeling that your body or environment is unreal; hot flashes or chills; chest pain or discomfort;

or unreasonable fear, such as fear of dying, going crazy, or losing self-control.

Another common anxiety disorder is phobia, which is an irrational avoidance of an object or situation that causes a lot of anxiety. Phobias sometimes are accompanied by panic attacks. Going out of the home, being in public, speaking in public, being closed in, or being in crowds are just a few of the situations that can trigger phobias. Phobias often constrict a person's life and cause serious problems.

If your anxious feelings are part of one of these, or other anxiety disorders, then you are advised to consult a mental health professional to help you determine the best treatment approach. You may not be able to deal with these disorders on your own, so seeking professional care is in your best interest. Without the proper treatment, you are more prone to relapse to your addiction because it is one way to handle your anxiety, panic, or phobic symptoms.

The list below presents some methods you can use to handle anxiety.

Practice challenging and changing your anxious thoughts or beliefs.

Find out specific problems or things that cause you to feel anxious and work on changing these when possible.

Evaluate your diet. Is your use of caffeine, tobacco, sugar, or other foods contributing to anxiety?

Evaluate your lifestyle. Are you getting sufficient rest, relaxation, and exercise?

Learn to meditate.

Learn relaxation techniques.

If your anxiety level continues to cause you significant distress, consult a mental health professional.

If your anxiety is a symptom of a psychiatric illness and does not decrease as a result of making some of these changes, you may benefit from medications. You should see a psychiatrist, psychologist, or other mental health professional if you have an illness requiring treatment.

BOREDOM

Stopping an addiction often leads to feeling a void or a sense of emptiness, which contributes to feelings of boredom. If much of your time and energy was directed toward your addiction, or if your lifestyle revolved around it, you are likely to feel very bored when you first give up your addiction. You may miss the "action" associated with your addiction, even if this action caused great difficulties in your life.

Boredom may also stem from a lack of important interests, activities, or relationships. As addiction progresses, it is not unusual for people to stop doing many things that had been enjoyable. Think back to the time before you had an addiction and answer these questions:

What interests, hobbies, or activities did you enjoy in the past that were not related to your addiction?

Which of these did you eventually give up as a result of your addiction?

Which of these do you miss the most?

Which of these would you like to rediscover as your recovery progresses?

Some people stop their addiction and evaluate their lives only to discover that they are bored with their jobs, marriages, or some other major aspects of their lives. This type of boredom differs from the boredom that accompanies early recovery. Decisions about your job or relationships should be thought out very carefully before major changes are made. A general rule of thumb followed by many people in recovery programs is to avoid making major life changes in the first year or so of recovery unless the change is made to help the recovery or is simply unavoidable. Think long and hard about making a major life change only because you are bored.

Feelings of boredom can lead to increased thoughts about your addictive habit. After all, your addiction did provide a sense of structure to your life. Perhaps it gave you something to do. Or perhaps it gave you a sense of adventure, even danger. If living on the edge made you feel alive, recovery will be quite a jolt to you at first. For some—particularly cocaine addicts and compulsive gamblers—recovery seems tiresome at first because it takes them away from the action. There are no magical fixes for this kind of boredom. You simply have to change your expectations, wait things out, and pay your dues in recovery. Eventually you should feel that the efforts were worth it.

A common response to boredom is filling up all of your free time with activities. Be careful of being too active. If you are always on the go and are constantly busy you can wear yourself out. Exhaustion can, in turn, lower your defenses and make you vulnerable to relapse. You can even get "too busy" to attend the meetings of your self-help group.

Some addicts find that they are more prone to boredom at certain times of the day or days of the week. For example, if weekends or evenings were the times you mainly participated in your addiction, then these are the times you are most likely to miss the addiction and feel restless or bored. A beginning step of recovery is identifying the most difficult times of the day or week. Then try to find out why these times are the most difficult. For example, Judy, a recovering drug addict, identified Friday and Saturday evenings as her most difficult times. "I was used to partying hard during these times. When I first got clean, I got real bored being away from the action. Then, I'd get restless and start scheming about how to sneak some drugs. I had to retrain myself about how I thought about the weekends. At first, the only thing I could do is go to NA [Narcotics Anonymous] meetings or visit family or clean friends. Eventually, I learned to keep busy at home, even if I am by myself. My boredom ain't as bad as it used to be. When I begin to scheme about coping some dope, I call my sponsor. Or, I ask myself why I want to throw away my recovery."

Another method of reducing boredom is to get into the habit of planning how to use your free time so that you have fun. You do not have to plan for every free minute. On the other hand, try to avoid not planning anything and flying by the seat of your pants. Take the initiative and plan some things you will enjoy that do not threaten your recovery.

Exploring new hobbies or interests is yet another way of dealing with boredom. What are some things you have always wanted to do but never got around to doing? You could choose one of these activities or interests and make plans to do it.

Involvement in meaningful experiences also reduces boredom. These experiences may relate to your religious beliefs and practices; to your artistic, musical, or athletic talent; or to helping others. Volunteering at hospitals, treatment clinics, or senior citizen programs helps some people feel like they are contributing something to the good of society. Such activities can give meaning to your life and cut down on boredom. A key issue here is getting outside of yourself and focusing on others.

A last method for dealing with boredom is to adjust your attitudes and beliefs. Kathy, a recovering sex addict, believed that "I had to be doing something exciting all of the time." She could not sit still very long without feeling quite bored. She expected herself always to be having a good time and involved in something exciting. This idea was quite unrealistic, because life is not always exciting. Kathy had to discover that a lack of activity now and then is just fine. In fact, it is even all right to feel bored from time to time. Although it was not easy by any means, Kathy had to learn to adjust her expectations about excitement. She did this in two ways: changing her thoughts to "I can do normal things and still enjoy them" and changing her behaviors. Kathy learned, for example, that a quiet visit with her mother, sitting quietly and reading a magazine, or baby-sitting her nephew and niece were ways of reducing her boredom. You have to enjoy the routine day-to-day activities of life; otherwise you set yourself up for relapse.

The list below presents some methods you can use to handle boredom.

Regain lost activities that you enjoyed prior to your addiction. Make sure these are not activities that threaten your ongoing recovery.

If you feel a need for high levels of action, excitement, and risk, gradually learn to enjoy simple, day-to-day pleasures. Do not expect always to be able to satisfy this need for action.

Learn new hobbies, develop new interests, or find new forms of pleasure or enjoyment.

Build fun into your day-to-day life. Try to find a balance between activities involving other people and those involving just yourself.

Identify high-risk times for feeling bored and plan activities as needed during some of these times.

Change your attitudes and beliefs about boredom. For example, expect some boredom and do not think you always have to be busy at something.

Focus your attention on meaningful relationships. If necessary, find new people to develop relationships with.

Carefully evaluate boredom with your relationships or job before making any major changes. Do not make quick or impulsive changes, especially major ones.

If you feel very empty inside and nothing seems to have meaning or purpose, consult a professional mental health therapist. You may benefit from therapy. This feeling sometimes is a symptom of a psychiatric illness such as depression.

DEPRESSION

Everyone feels "down in the dumps," "blue," "bummed out," or depressed from time to time. Such feelings are a fairly natural part of life. Many different things happen to us to make us feel this way. This normal feeling of depression usually does not cause a great deal of distress or interfere with our lives.

However, there is another more serious type of depression called clinical depression. Many of us experience one or more episodes of clinical depression at some time in our lives. This type of depression is more serious than the everyday blues that we all get and it often persists for several weeks or longer. Clinical depression often causes a great deal of personal suffering and can disrupt a person's life. Some people suffer many episodes of clinical depression; some people even feel depressed throughout most of their lives.

Research shows that depression is more common among people with certain types of addictive diseases. Depression may result from the effects of addictive substances, such as alcohol or other drugs, or from the losses associated with an addiction—loss of relationships, a job, money, status, or self-esteem, to name just a few. Sometimes depression is a clinical disorder that is independent of the addiction. This type of depression should be evaluated and treated by a mental health professional, usually a psychiatrist, psychologist, or other specialist. When medications are used, they must be taken under the supervision of a psychiatrist.

You can deal with feelings of depression in a variety of ways. The results may vary from significant improvement and a resolution of depression to a mild decrease in depression. You should always work at improvement, even if it comes in very small steps. Expecting too much too soon can set you up to feel bad about yourself.

One way of decreasing depression is to identify the problems or issues causing you to feel depressed and then do something about them. Sometimes these problems are connected to your addiction. For example, Liz felt depressed because of serious financial and family problems caused by her many years of compulsive gambling. She did not feel better until she began putting her life back together. She not only had to stop gambling entirely, but she had to figure out ways to deal with her financial difficulties, make amends to her family for causing them so much trouble, and get settled in a new job. In short, she had to slowly put the pieces of her life back together again. As things gradually got better, she felt less depressed and better about herself. It would have been unrealistic for her to expect her feelings of depression to leave quickly because of the many serious problems caused by her compulsive gambling.

In other cases, problems that upset or depress you may have nothing to do with your addictive habit. Michael, for example, felt depressed because he hated his job. Going to work was a chore for him because it brought him no satisfaction whatsoever. When he finally accepted the fact that his work was not suited to his interests and abilities, he was able to begin looking for a new job. He eventually landed a more suitable job and felt much less depressed. Going to work became enjoyable for him.

Another way to help decrease your depression is to talk about your feelings. Many of us let our feelings build up, and this can contribute to depression. Many feelings are associated with depression and simply venting them through discussion can provide some relief. Such feelings include sadness, guilt, shame, powerlessness, and anger.

Some experts believe that turning too much anger inward can make you feel depressed. Others believe that holding on to past hurts or emotional pains can contribute to depression. Perhaps you were a victim of physical or sexual abuse when you grew up and you still have bad memories and painful feelings about these experiences. Maybe you feel you were deprived of a childhood because you grew up with parents who were addicted or mentally ill. Or perhaps you lost important people as a result of death or some other reason and you were not able to grieve about these losses.

Sometimes talking about such feelings is enough to give you relief from them. After many years, David finally allowed himself to feel sad and cry over the death of his grandfather. He initially had dealt with his grandfather's death quite intellectually and had pushed back his true feelings. Albert let go of a lot of anger toward his father that had built up for many years. Even though his father had been dead for several years, acknowledging and expressing his feelings allowed Albert to feel better.

At other times, talking about your feelings allows you to think more clearly about different options you have for dealing with them. For example, when Liz (the compulsive gambler mentioned earlier) talked about her anger at herself, it opened the door for self-forgiveness and acceptance. She was then able to be more realistic about her anger at her mother. For years she had denied and swallowed her angry feelings. Only when she began to admit these feelings was she able to feel better about herself. A result was feeling less depressed.

Experts such as Dr. Aaron Beck, Dr. David Burns, and Dr. Albert Ellis have taught us that depressed thoughts can contribute to depressed feelings. By changing negative or depressed thoughts, or the beliefs and assumptions upon which these thoughts are based, you can make yourself feel better and less depressed. For example, Katie was self-critical and felt depressed because she had put ten pounds back on. She berated herself for being a failure at keeping her weight down, despite the fact that in the past two years she had dropped over eighty pounds. Her belief that she had to be perfect and should never re-gain any weight set her up to feel failure when she put a few pounds back on. This in turn led to feeling depressed. However, Katie challenged this false belief and told herself, "I fell back a little and made a mistake, but this doesn't mean the end of the world." This helped her put things in better perspective. A result was feeling less depressed.

Although discussed in greater detail in the next chapter, "Overcoming Negative Thinking," it is worthwhile to mention some common examples of thinking that may contribute to depressed feelings. Such thoughts include

Expecting the worst outcome.

Making mountains out of molehills.

Focusing only on the negative and ignoring the positive.

Berating yourself for making a mistake.

Expecting perfection and ignoring progress, even small steps.

Reaching a conclusion based on insufficient evidence.

Learning about these and other common distortions of thinking not only can help your recovery, but are a great way to lessen feelings of depression.

Getting active can help take your mind off of your depression. Taking a shower, cleaning up your apartment or house, going for a walk, reading a book, calling a friend, going to a movie, working at a hobby, or going shopping are just a few of many actions you can take to get yourself moving. Tom said that whenever he began to feel depressed and did not want to do anything he knew he needed to push himself to take action. "Hard as it was at times," he said, "the better it made me feel in the long run." Sometimes you need to push yourself the most when you feel least like doing anything.

Some people find it helpful to plan pleasant activities. These provide enjoyment and can take your mind off of depression. You need to find pleasant activities. Forcing yourself to participate in such activities may be necessary at first because your depression may lead you to avoid anything pleasant.

Physical activity can help you feel better. Regular exercise, participation in sports, or other forms of physical exertion can help decrease depression. Force yourself if you have to, but try to be active in some type of physical endeavor.

Evaluating your relationships with other people may be a key issue in depression. If you have few or no relationships, or they are characterized by serious problems or conflicts, you are more likely to feel depressed. If your needs for love, intimacy, closeness, and connection with others are not met, you are probably more susceptible to depression. Since addiction commonly creates serious problems in relationships with family members and loved ones, you need to look at what you can do to repair some of the damage and make things better in these relationships.

Sometimes you may need professional help for depression. Here are some indicators that your depression should be evaluated by a professional:

It continues for several weeks or longer and does not seem to improve.

It continues even though you try many of the coping strategies discussed previously.

You have serious thoughts about taking your life.

You have an actual plan to take your life or have made an attempt.

It interferes with your ability to function (at home, work, school, and so on) or to take care of yourself.

It causes you significant personal suffering.

Other people think you need help because you are not yourself and do not seem to be getting better on your own.

Some types of depression will only get better with the use of antidepressant medications. Medications are usually used in addition to personal therapy. You should not feel guilty if you need an antidepressant medication. While some people are able to benefit from the short-term use of these medicines, others may need them for years. The amount of time depends on the particular symptoms of your depression, how long you have had them, and whether you have what is called recurrent depression. Some people are susceptible to recurrent episodes of depression.

Medications may help reduce the likelihood of future episodes or reduce the severity of the episodes.

The following list presents some methods you can use to handle depression.

Identify the problems that are causing your depression and do something about them.

Make amends to significant people whom you feel you hurt because of your addiction.

Evaluate your relationships with other people. Develop new relationships and change problematic ones. Look at whether your needs are satisfied by your current relationships.

Keep active, even if you have to force yourself to do things. When you least want to do things may be when you most need to.

Talk about your feelings and problems with others. Look for feelings that may contribute to depression, such as anger, guilt, or shame.

Learn to challenge and change your negative or depressing thoughts.

Participate in pleasant activities each day.

If your depression does not get better, seek an evaluation by a mental health professional. Some types of depression require the use of antidepressant medications.

GUILT AND SHAME

Feelings of guilt and shame go hand in hand with addictive diseases and addictive habits. Guilt refers to feeling bad about your actions or inactions—things that you did or failed to do. For example, Lorraine was very irresponsible in many ways in her relationships with family and friends. She lied, stole, borrowed money that never was repaid, and said and did things to hurt others. Lorraine was manipulative and self-centered during her active addiction. Her parents were deeply hurt because Lorraine called or visited them only when she seemed to want something from them. Addiction often causes people to do many things to hurt others. The things that Lorraine did are just a few examples of many kinds of behavior that cause guilt.

Shame refers to feeling bad about yourself because you have an addiction. You feel defective, or like a failure. You believe that something is wrong with you rather than with your behaviors.

Overcoming shame and guilt will take time in recovery. There is no shortcut through these feelings. This process is a gradual one that begins with an honest acceptance of your addiction. You must admit and believe that you are powerless over your addiction and that it controlled your life. Your addiction impaired your judgment so that you did things that hurt others. Accept that you are not bad even though some of your behaviors were bad and harmful.

You must come to see addiction as causing your life to become unmanageable. Admit the ways in which it had a negative impact on your life as well as on the lives of others. Talk about what you did or failed to do with others, particularly with others recovering from addiction. Sometimes a private discussion with a sponsor, minister, priest, rabbi, or other trusted person is necessary to reduce your guilt.

Seeing yourself as addicted rather than bad can help reduce your shame. Everyone has defects, limitations, and problems. You must come to grips with this fact to establish long-term recovery.

Talking about your sense of self and your shame with others who accept you can aid the healing process. Acceptance by others, despite all of your limitations, can be a potent force in recovery.

For many, a belief in and reliance on God or another higher power is the key to getting over guilt and shame. Do not underestimate the power that praying and participating in religious activities can have. The self-help programs work well because they address guilt and shame as well as other spiritual issues.

Using the twelve-step program advocated by most self-help organizations provides you with an opportunity to resolve your guilt and shame. Many of the steps focus on these issues in a variety of ways. The love and acceptance you feel in the fellowship can be extremely powerful in your recovery. (A list of the self-help organizations dealing with the different types of addiction is given at the end of the book.)

The following list presents some methods you can use to reduce guilt and shame. By answering these questions and discussing these issues with a person whom you trust, you can begin healing your feelings of guilt and shame.

What have you done during your addiction, or what have you failed to do, that you feel guilty about?

Have you discussed with others the things you have done or failed to do that made you feel guilty? If yes, what were the results? If not, why not?

Do you feel defective, bad, or shameful?

How would you describe your sense of shame about yourself?

In whose presence do you feel the most shame? Why?

Have you made amends to others hurt by your addiction? If yes, what were the results of this process? If not, why not?

Do you believe in God or a power greater than yourself?

6

Overcoming Negative Thinking

FOR many years, philosophers, poets, and psychologists have written about how our thinking influences every aspect of our lives. Self-destructive or negative thinking patterns are associated with many human ailments. Such ailments include not only addictive disorders, but mental health problems such as depression, anxiety, antisocial behavior, and low self-esteem. There is little doubt that thinking exerts a powerful influence on our lives.

Our thoughts affect the emotions we experience. Anger, sadness, anxiety, excitement, and many other feelings—both negative and positive—are connected with our thinking. How we act is also affected by our thinking. Indeed, our happiness or unhappiness can be traced to the ways in which we think about ourselves, our lives, our relationships with other people, and the future.

We can talk ourselves into virtually anything, from feeling satisfied about an accomplishment to taking a risk by changing jobs. Consider the college student who worked extremely hard at mathematics only to earn a grade C. Positive thinking allows her to feel quite satisfied with this grade because mathematics has always been a very difficult subject for her and she knows she worked very hard to get even an average grade.

On the other hand, we can talk ourselves out of anything, even out of feeling satisfied about an important accomplishment. Consider the man who gets a well-deserved promotion because of his hard work but is unable to appreciate his accomplishment.

When he begins to feel a sense of satisfaction or pride, he questions whether or not he really deserves the promotion. His thinking causes him to have a negative outlook on a positive event. He feels anxious and frustrated as a result and cannot enjoy his promotion.

Negative thinking often causes problems during recovery from an addiction. "Addictive thinking" or "stinking thinking" are just two of the many terms used to describe such thinking. Addictive thinking refers to self-defeating or faulty statements (called "self-statements") that you make to yourself or your beliefs about yourself, your relationships, the future, your addiction, and your recovery.

Addictive thinking not only affects your recovery, but also your happiness as a person. Paying attention to your specific thoughts or internal messages, or to the beliefs that underlie them, can help you gain better control of them. This control allows you to challenge faulty or self-destructive thinking. Disputing these ideas, in turn, makes it much easier to accept your mistakes and learn from experience. The result of identifying, challenging, and changing your thinking can be more control over your emotions, behaviors, and life. Recovery will go more smoothly then.

In the sections that follow I discuss common beliefs and other distortions of thinking that can cause problems in your recovery. I will also give you some ideas about how to cope with them.

Thoughts and Beliefs

Thoughts are automatic and pop into your head—often you are not aware of where they come from. Your beliefs influence your specific thoughts and patterns of thinking. Your beliefs guide your behavior, even though you are probably not aware of them when you act. For example, Jim experienced a strong craving for cocaine. He thought about how good he would feel "if I snorted a couple lines of coke." The longer he craved drugs, the worse he began to feel about himself because he had been drug-free for over one year. Jim believed he was a "hopeless addict who would always be controlled by hunger for drugs. After all, I've been clean for a long time." It was not until he caught himself in this downward spiral of negative thinking that Jim could change how he felt. He challenged his distorted notion that he was hopeless by saying to himself, "Just because I have a desire for drugs doesn't mean I have to give in to it. And, it doesn't mean I'm hopeless. This isn't the first time I've had drug hunger and it probably won't be the last time, either. Most cocaine addicts think about getting high again. It comes with addiction." Had Jim not challenged his belief about being a "hopeless addict" he would have been at higher risk of relapse.

Sylvia was hosting her first dinner party since starting her recovery from compulsive overeating. She was known for providing outstanding feasts for her guests, who were very well fed from the many hors d'oeuvres to the exotic desserts. When first planning the menu for the dinner party, Sylvia began to feel depressed and guilty because she was trying a new approach to hosting dinner parties. This new approach called for her to cut back on the number of hors d'oeuvres and courses served. Sylvia thought, "This dinner is going to be a disaster." She believed that the number of courses she served was a reflection of her competence as a cook and value as a person, and had a direct bearing on how much enjoyment her guests would get from her dinner. A related belief was that the dinner itself was the most important part of the evening, not the socializing with good friends. To change her feelings, Sylvia had to tell herself, "Just because I'm not serving several different hors d'oeuvres and six courses doesn't mean I'm not a good cook or we can't have an excellent meal." She had to challenge her faulty beliefs and accept the fact that the number of food items served had no bearing on her competence and on her guests' ultimate enjoyment of the evening. Sylvia also had to remind herself that the meal was just one part of the evening, that sharing time with good friends was much more important than what people ate or how many courses she prepared.

Beliefs that guide your behavior and affect your feelings usually fall into one of several categories. These include beliefs about

yourself and your capabilities,

relationships with other people,

events in your life,

the future,

addiction,

recovery, and

relapse.

Beliefs about Yourself and Your Capabilities

Many individuals with an addiction believe they are bad or unworthy people. They have low opinions of themselves and low self-esteem. As a result, they feel shameful or defective, like "damaged goods." Some even feel unlovable. In spite of evidence to the contrary, they may feel inadequate and downplay their talents, achievements, or capabilities. They may see their weaknesses and deficits more clearly than their strengths. Some people cannot even acknowledge any personal strengths or achievements. On the other hand, some people are just the opposite in their thinking about themselves. They have an exaggerated and distorted positive view of themselves. They think much too highly of themselves or of what they are capable of doing. In either case, how addicted people view themselves and their capabilities can affect their ability to recover from their addictive disorders.

Some examples of self-defeating beliefs include:

I'll never be able to kick my addiction.

I'll probably relapse; my addiction just is too strong for me to handle.

I'm a weak person.

I'll never succeed in life.

I can't handle this problem.

I can't go back to school; it's been too long. I'll probably fail.

I'm a bad person for having an addiction.

Suppose that a compulsive gambler believes she is "not capable of recovery" because she relapsed and went on a weekend gambling trip. With such a belief, she is less likely to approach the challenges of recovery in a confident and positive way. Instead, she will view herself as a helpless victim controlled by some external force. As a consequence, she may not put forth her best efforts because she believes that she is not capable of doing well in recovery.

Alternatively, suppose that a man believes he can control his impulses to engage in harmful, self-destructive compulsive sexual behaviors. In this case, he is more likely to control these impulses. His positive belief in himself will help him even when such impulses for sex are quite strong. The issue is not so much whether or not he has an impulse to engage in sex, but what he does to handle his impulse in a way that is healthy and allows him to prevent a relapse.

BELIEFS ABOUT YOUR RELATIONSHIPS

One of the most important areas of your life centers on your relationships with your family and other people. People who have satisfying interpersonal relationships are usually happier than those who do not. The satisfaction you get from your particular relationships will be affected by your beliefs and your behaviors. So will your feelings about people.

Faulty beliefs have the potential to cause problems in your personal relationships with others. A few examples of such beliefs about relationships include:

I have to be accepted by everybody.

Conflict or anger is to be avoided at all costs.

What other people think about me ultimately determines my value as a human being.

I'll lose all or most of my friends if I stop my addiction.

I won't fit in anymore and my friends will think I'm square.

I'll never be able to depend on others to get my needs met.

If I show you the real person I am, you won't like me.

For example, if an alcoholic believes that his needs are the most important ones to be satisfied in relationships, then his relationships are likely to be one-sided and centered on him. He is more prone to turning people off or pushing them away because of his self-centeredness. And he is more likely to attract people who have tremendous needs to take care of and cater to people like himself. In this case, the alcoholic's relationships will be problematic, even if he does not admit this.

BELIEFS ABOUT EVENTS IN YOUR LIFE

More often than not, what happens in your life is not what dictates how you feel or act; rather, it is what you believe about these events. Take, for example, two people who worked together and lost their jobs because the company they worked for went bankrupt. One person sees this as a rather unfortunate event that was out of his control. He is upset and sad because the company folded but immediately reviews his options and begins to plot out where to find work. He views this as an opportunity to find a better or more interesting job. The other person is extremely angry and depressed. She feels cheated and bitter. She believes that "I should have known better than to work for such a second-rate company. What was wrong with me for taking a job with them in the first place?" She obsesses about the uncertainty of her future. "What am I going to do? Who will want me?" are a few of the questions showing her self-doubt. She is so distraught and her confidence is so low that she cannot pull herself together to write a personal résumé or look for a new job. In these two cases, it is not so much losing the jobs as the individuals' interpretation and self-talk that determined how they handled the same situation in entirely different manners.

It is common for addicted people to use unfortunate life events as excuses to engage in the addictive behavior. "Why not binge on food, I lost my job?" "I didn't get the new job I wanted, so I deserve a reward [alcohol, drugs, some gambling action, compulsive sex, or forbidden food]." "Everything is going to pot, my car needs fixing, my kids are doing bad in school, and my taxes are overdue, so I might as well get drunk." Such statements are but a few examples of negative thoughts about life events or circumstances.

On the other hand, some people will use positive life events as a reason to engage in their addictive habits. Getting a promotion or receiving money unexpectedly can lead you to feel like a celebration is in order. And what better way to celebrate than to allow yourself to go back to your addiction—a drug, alcohol, food, gambling, or sex binge?

BELIEFS ABOUT YOUR FUTURE

The more time you spend worrying about situations or events that may happen in the future, the greater your level of anxiety. The higher your anxiety level gets, the more at risk you are to engage in your addictive habit. One of the functions of addiction is to control anxious feelings in the short run. In the long run, however, addiction usually raises your level of anxiety.

Two typical faulty beliefs about the future are: "I don't have any control over what will happen in the future" and "I can control all or most of what happens in my future." The reality is that you have some control over your future. If, for example, you set goals for the future and work toward them, you have a chance of reaching them. This proactive stance will make you feel a greater sense of control over your life, even if there are limitations to what you can actually control. On the other hand, if you believe the future is totally out of your control, you may choose not to set any future goals. You will probably feel too helpless to have a say about what happens in your future. This passive stance will be a major factor in causing dissatisfaction and feelings of unhappiness in your life.

BELIEFS ABOUT YOUR ADDICTION

Your view of addiction influences how you approach recovery. If addiction seems like a simple matter to you, you may get complacent and lazy and be taken by surprise by the challenges of recovery. If you believe that your addiction "is no big deal," "is caused by a lack of willpower," or "can easily be explained," then you may set yourself up to fail. If you see addiction primarily from one point of view—physiological, psychological, environmental, or spiritual—you may ignore the role of multiple factors in causing addiction.

How you view your addiction also determines the amount of effort you put into recovery. A very common irrational and self-defeating belief associated with addiction is "Alcohol [drugs, sex, food, gambling] is my most important need, and I can't live without it." This helps to explain why some people go to any lengths to engage in their addictive habits, even when it causes a great deal of difficulty in their lives. Those who believe that their addiction is a major threat to their lives and well-being are usually the people who approach recovery most seriously. Such people work harder at getting well.

BELIEFS ABOUT YOUR RECOVERY

Another very common self-defeating belief is that recovery is simply not engaging in the addictive behavior. While this is a very important element of recovery, abstinence from the substance or behavior is not all that is needed to get well. Change is also required. Those who believe that stopping the addictive habit is enough quite often are surprised when they realize there is much more to getting well. They may also be more prone to relapse because they do not make the changes necessary to support abstinence from addictive behavior.

Other common self-defeating beliefs about recovery include:

Recovery is easy and does not require much effort.

Stopping my addictive habit is all I need to do. I don't need to change anything else.

Recovery is boring or will make my life dull.

Change is just too damn hard to make.

Recovery is going too slowly.

If you have unrealistic expectations about recovery and believe that things must always go well, you set yourself up to feel bad when you struggle with a conflict or when things are not going well. If you believe that recovery is an ongoing, active experience requiring time, effort, and commitment, you put yourself in a better position to make the positive changes necessary to support your recovery.

BELIEFS ABOUT RELAPSE

Beliefs about relapse can affect whether or not it happens to you, as well as how you respond if you return to your addictive habit. Common self-defeating beliefs regarding relapse are:

I will never overeat [drink, take drugs, gamble, engage in compulsive sex] again.

Relapse cannot happen to me.

As long as I am motivated to recover, I cannot relapse.

I have learned my lesson, so I could never relapse.

Such beliefs may accompany a strong recovery plan and a great personal desire to change your addiction. However, a good recovery plan and strong motivation do not make you immune from relapse. In many cases, people have relapsed after many years in a recovery program.

Believing the addictive substance or habit is needed to "have fun," "make me feel alive," "reduce stress," or "make problems go away" are other self-defeating beliefs that set you up for relapse. In addition, a false sense of control over your addiction and the belief that you can control yourself by taking only a few drinks (or waging a few bets) put you at risk for relapse.

Faulty beliefs can also occur after you return to your addictive habit. Brad, an overweight man who had eaten compulsively for over twenty years, started the Overeaters Anonymous program and personal therapy. He worked hard and lost over one hundred pounds. When he regained four pounds during the Christmas holidays he judged himself quite harshly and began to view himself as a failure. Brad not only had lost quite a bit of weight, but had made a number of substantial changes in his attitudes, personality, and lifestyle. Yet he was quick to brush aside his progress because of his distorted belief that regaining a few pounds meant that he was a failure. To get back on the right track, Brad had to remind himself that he was seeking progress, not perfection, and that he was not a failure because of gaining four pounds. After all, he had come a long way to reach this point!

Common Distortions of Thinking

Dr. Aaron Beck and Dr. David Burns, two well-known psychiatrists, and Dr. Albert Ellis, a well-known psychologist, have noted that some fairly typical distortions of thinking are associated with depression, anxiety, and other human problems. Part of treatment for depression, anxiety, or other problems involves becoming aware of and changing how you think. The types of thinking errors these experts have written about are common among people with addictive disorders. As you go through the following list, identify the faulty ideas that relate to you and pose a risk to your ongoing recovery.

BLACK-AND-WHITE THINKING

Seeing things in terms of all or none, right or wrong, yes or no is black-and-white thinking. Things are either one way or the other; there are no grey areas with this type of thinking. Such a rigid stance gives you little room for flexibility. Examples of black-and-white thinking include:

My recovery either goes well or poorly.

All AA meetings are boring.

All men [or women] are out to take advantage of me.

Everyone is out to get what they can from me.

No one is honest anymore.

You cannot trust any addict.

People either like you or they do not like you.

Jack, a member of a self-help program for sex addicts, was told by his sponsor that his attitude toward recovery was becoming negative. Jack's response to this was to think "he's criticizing me, he doesn't like me." Jack felt accepted and liked by his sponsor most of the time but at times like this, when his sponsor gave him critical feedback, Jack immediately took it to mean that his sponsor disliked him. Jack had to stop thinking that his sponsor either liked or disliked him. He had to learn to evaluate his sponsor's attitude in terms of degrees. Jack told himself, "He's telling me these things because he wants to help me. This isn't something someone would do if they didn't care about you." Viewing situations on a continuum, in terms of degrees rather than absolutes, can help you learn to correct this type of mistaken thinking.

EXAGGERATING PROBLEMS

Making mountains out of molehills and turning minor inconveniences into major problems characterize exaggerated thinking. You may focus too much on one negative detail of a situation and let this detail dictate how you perceive the entire situation. Kathy, a recovering overeater, got caught in a big traffic jam. It was clear that she would be late for work. At first, she told herself, "It's going to be one of those rotten days when everything goes wrong." But Kathy caught herself and asked herself this simple question: "How does getting caught in traffic prove that the entire day will be screwed up?" She told herself, "I might as well make the best of it," and listened to music and plotted out her day at work. Kathy also was able to handle her frustrations without eating in the car. "In the past, I would have dealt with my irritations by eating my lunch. Of course, this would have allowed me to buy another lunch at work. So I would have gotten two lunches just because of a little old traffic jam!"

If you evaluate an entire situation realistically, you will be better able to avoid making things worse than they really are. Look at the big picture rather than at a single, negative detail.

OVERGENERALIZING

When you reach a general conclusion based on a single experience you are overgeneralizing. Natalie, a compulsive gambler, was not chosen for a job that she felt very qualified for. Based on this rejection she thought, "No one wants to hire me," and so she felt depressed and dejected. Natalie did not feel better until she said to herself, "Wait a minute, that was only one job interview. I have a long history of success at getting jobs, and there are a lot of employers who would want me. Besides, nobody gets every job they want."

Diane, a heroin addict, impulsively got high when an old friend stopped by unexpectedly with a stash of drugs. She offered drugs to Diane, who gave in to this pressure and used drugs on just this one occasion. Initially, Diane interpreted her this one episode to mean that she was a total failure. But this woman, prior to getting involved in recovery, had shot large amounts of drugs into her veins every single day! To counteract this distorted thinking, Diane had to remind herself that she had made only a single mistake, but that she needed to get hold of herself to prevent a full-blown relapse.

Curtis had a disagreement with a coworker. His immediate response was, "I can't work with this guy. He's too difficult to get along with." Curtis quickly caught this thinking error when he reminded himself he and this coworker had gotten along fine for most of the five years that they had worked together.

You can counteract the thinking error of overgeneralizing by looking at the faulty logic behind reaching a broad conclusion based on evidence from only one experience. Remind yourself that generalizations cannot be made accurately from a single experience.

EXPECTING THE WORST

Another fairly common thinking error is expecting the worst to happen. This expectation ignores all of the possible outcomes of a situation. A few examples in which people assume that the worst thing will happen include:

I am not going to get my promotion.

My husband is going to be very angry with me because I hit another car and put a dent in our car.

My wife will be very disappointed when she finds out I put a few pounds back on.

Everybody is going to be upset and mad at me because I got high once.

Such distorted thinking also can affect feeling upset, depressed, or anxious. This thinking error magnifies your problems and creates catastrophies by focusing on very negative outcomes of situations. The terrible outcome you may expect often does not actually occur.

When you think the worst-case scenario will happen, ask yourself, "Why do I think the worst will happen?" "What proof do I have?" or "Why am I magnifying the situation?" For example, Carol, a recovering gambler, took care of the budget for her family. Recently, when paying bills for the month, she discovered that they were about two hundred dollars short. Many unexpected expenses had occurred, throwing her budget off target. Carol became quite worried that her husband would be upset and blame her. Because her husband was also a recovering gambler, she worried that he might use this shortfall as an excuse to relapse to gambling. Fortunately, Carol caught herself before her thinking became too irrational. She thought, "Wait a minute. Frank knows we had extra medical expenses this month. Why would he be upset with me for something I didn't have any control over? He's usually very reasonable about things like this. He's been doing well in recovery and I know he doesn't want to mess that up, so thinking that he'd be upset and gamble doesn't make sense. Hey, maybe this situation isn't as bad as I think. I'll talk with Frank tonight about how we can handle this problem. I know we can figure something out."

IGNORING THE POSITIVE

Another type of thinking error allows you to overlook or minimize the positive achievements, successes, or personality traits of yourself or others. You tend to ignore the positive and see the negative, even if there is really very little negative in a situation.

Richard, who was recovering from compulsive sexual behaviors, worked hard at dealing with his guilt and shame, his anger, and his family relationships. He made excellent progress in his recovery. Once, however, he lost his temper and lashed out at his wife and sons. Afterward, Richard berated himself for getting angry and shouting at his family. He thought he was doing poorly in recovery because of this incident. How quickly he forgot all of the times he had dealt with his anger in a positive fashion!

By ignoring his positive changes and focusing on one mistake, Richard lost his perspective for a while, which caused him to feel anxious and upset with himself. Fortunately, he caught himself before things got too distorted. "I admitted I made a mistake and handled the situation poorly by lashing out. But, I have to keep in mind I've made good progress. No one is perfect. Mistakes will be made. I'll apologize to my family and try harder not to jump on them in the future."

Looking for the positive aspects of a situation can help you counter this type of distorted thinking. Even difficult or problematic situations often have some positive aspect if you look hard enough. Periodically reviewing positive aspects of your life and reminding yourself of things you do well and positive personality traits can also help you correct this problem.

JUMPING TO CONCLUSIONS

When you reach a negative or incorrect judgment before you have the facts of a situation, you are reacting too quickly and impulsively jumping to a wrong conclusion.

Bennett thought that a fellow Gamblers Anonymous member was upset and angry with him, or maybe did not like him, because this man had not been as friendly as usual during the past several meetings. In fact, after the last meeting his friend had declined Bennett's invitation to go out for a cup of coffee. Bennett felt quite upset because he liked this man and valued his opinions. "It really bothered me that I got the cold shoulder," he said. However, it turned out that Bennett's friend had been going through a difficult time with an ill family member and was feeling preoccupied and depressed as a result. This accounted for his mood and behavior changes. When Bennett found out, he changed the faulty conclusions he had previously reached. He was then able to reach out and offer some support to his friend during this difficult period rather than jumping to the conclusion that his friend was angry with him or no longer liked him.

Ann is usually a friendly, happy-go-lucky person. She is well liked by others and her positive attitude and approach to people is refreshing to many of her colleagues and friends. But for a time, Ann was not her usual self. She was rather subdued and quiet, and not as outgoing and friendly as usual. Her husband

Gene thought she was upset and angry with him. He could not understand because, to the best of his knowledge, he had not done anything to upset her. When Gene asked her if he had done something to make her angry, he learned that her mood had nothing whatsoever to do with him. In this case, his conclusion that "My wife is upset with me because she's quiet and not as friendly as usual" was reached quickly and prematurely, before he knew all of the facts.

The best way to avoid reaching premature conclusions is to get the facts of the situation. Investigate before you make a final judgment. Try not to read the behavior or moods of other people the wrong way.

EMOTIONAL RESPONSES

Another kind of thinking error occurs when you assume that your negative emotions reflect reality. As a result, you make harsh judgments about yourself and believe this feeling reflects a permanent part of your personality. Some examples are:

I feel worthless, so I must be worthless.

I feel like a failure, so I am a failure.

I feel inadequate (or incompetent), so I must be inadequate (or incompetent).

She is upset and disappointed with me. I am incompetent and a big disappointment.

Learning to separate a feeling from a self-judgment can help you counteract this type of distorted thinking. For example, you may say something like "I feel inadequate because I didn't really do a good job. But this doesn't mean that I'm an inadequate person." Keep in mind that your emotions reflect how you feel at a given time, not who or what you are as a person.

"SHOULD" OR "MUST" STATEMENTS

You set yourself up to feel bad when you try to follow too many "should" or "must" rules. Howard thought, "I should always

enjoy Overeaters Anonymous meetings because they help me."
He felt bad after meetings that he did not particularly enjoy or
benefit from. Howard felt better when he changed his thinking:
"The reality is, no matter how motivated I am, there will be times
in which I won't enjoy self-help meetings. They still help me,
even if sometimes I don't like certain meetings."

Other examples of this type of thinking error include:

Others should always treat me fairly.

I should always feel good about my husband [wife, child,
parent].

I must always be kind and patient.

I shouldn't take a vacation. I have too much work to do.

I should be nice to everyone.

I should always work very hard.

Give yourself a break and try not to let your "shoulds" and
"musts" dictate your feelings and behaviors. When you hear these
words in your thoughts, challenge them immediately. For example, Nancy was writing a book about her work with children.
At first, she was frustrated with herself because she repeatedly
told herself, "I should write for at least two hours every day."
Nancy also told herself, "I should be finished with this book in
six months." Her "shoulds" only led to frustration, because she
was unable to stick to her plan to write every day or to finish
her book in just six months. When Nancy changed her expectations and became more realistic, she felt better.

MISLABELING

Another type of distorted thinking leads you to create a negative
image of yourself that is based on your mistakes. You focus on
yourself as a person rather than on your behavior or actions.
With mislabeling, you interpret making a mistake as being a
mistake yourself. As a result, you say things like "I'm a failure"
instead of "I failed at something, or I made a mistake." Mislabeling often happens when an addicted person relapses. He or

she says things like "I'm a total failure, incapable of recovery," "I'm a terrible person because I relapsed," or "I'll always be a screw up."

Try not to label yourself as a failure, weak, or inadequate in response to a mistake. If you mislabel yourself in response to a mistake or a failure, ask yourself, "What warrants this harsh self-judgment?"

PERSONALIZING

Taking responsibility for negative events for which you are not responsible is another common thinking error. John blamed himself because his twenty-two-year-old son is an alcoholic. "I must have been a lousy father if my son developed alcoholism." John felt very guilty as a result. In order to feel good about himself, he had to dispute this belief with statements such as "I really did the best I could. It doesn't do any good to cast blame. You can be the best parent in the world and your kid can get hooked. There are lots of factors involved here, not just one."

Methods for Changing Your Thinking

COUNTERSTATEMENTS

One useful technique for changing your thinking is to find counterstatements that disprove your self-defeating statements. The examples that follow illustrate common negative ideas and show useful counterstatements.

Example 1

Self-defeating statement: I don't have the strength to get control of my overeating; maybe I'll never stop overeating and I'll always be way too fat.

Counterstatements:

1. Never is a long time. I'll work hard at making small steps toward progress. Little by little, things can improve. Even one pound at a time can help.

2. They say that recovery takes time and effort and it's not easy for anyone, especially at first. Until I feel stronger, I'll reach

out to others for help. My husband and Overeaters Anonymous sponsor said they would support me.

3. There have been times in the past when I stopped binging. I even lost a lot of weight on a couple of occasions. If I did it before, I can do it again.

Example 2

Self-defeating statement: My friends will think I'm square if I don't party and get loaded with them anymore.

Counterstatements:

1. What makes me think they expect me to get high with them? Maybe I'm really worried about fitting in. Besides, not all my friends abuse drugs.
2. If my friends think I'm square, that's just too bad. I can't control what they think.
3. I'd rather be square and clean than lose my sobriety and get loaded.

Example 3

Self-defeating statement: It's going to be a drag not being in the middle of some action. I know I'll get bored if I can't gamble.

Counterstatements:

1. I might miss the action for a while. But will I miss being in debt or messing up my life for gambling?
2. Things will get better. I just have to find some new things to do.
3. There're really a lot of things I enjoy doing that have nothing to do with gambling. I've always had a lot of interests.

Example 4

Self-defeating statement: What harm would come if I had sex with another person? I can control my impulses and won't let things get out of control this time. Besides, I'm bored with my wife.

Counterstatements:

1. I wonder why my addictive thinking is returning now? Most couples get bored with each other from time to time. What's really going on with me that I'm now feeling the need to act out again with another woman?

2. How in the hell could I even wonder what harm would come of it? I hurt my wife terribly in the past, not to mention myself.

3. My history has taught me that my impulses get out of control eventually, even if not at first. I have too much to lose by giving in.

Self-Awareness Task 6–1: *Overcoming Negative Thinking*

1. Review the examples of self-defeating beliefs and common thinking distortions discussed in this chapter. Make a list of all of those that you identify with.
2. Add your own self-defeating thoughts that were not discussed.
3. List (a) your beliefs, in categories covering yourself and your capabilities, your relationships, events in your life, your view of the future, addiction, recovery, and relapse; and (b) your habitual thinking errors.
4. Review your final list. Choose the five items that most threaten your recovery or your mental well-being. List these five in order, from the most bothersome to the least.
5. Practice countering each one of your negative thoughts by asking yourself, first, "What is my mistaken thought or distortion?" and, second, "What are two or more counterstatements I can use to change this self-defeating thought?"
6. Review the examples in this section that illustrate how to counter negative thinking. Learn what you can from these cases and from the experiences of others in recovery.

ACTIVITIES AND TECHNIQUES

Identifying and challenging self-defeating thoughts or beliefs takes time and practice. The longer you do this, however, the easier it becomes. In addition to using the approaches described previously, you can work on changing your thinking in other ways. A few of these are described in the following sections.

Keep a Written Journal. On a regular basis, keep track of your self-defeating thoughts and beliefs. Write down what they are, where you think they originated, the situations in which they occurred, the feelings they caused, and your counterstatements. It would be impractical to record all of your thoughts, so you may just wish to focus on several each day. Choose thoughts you want to work on countering.

Carry Practice Cards. Write one self-defeating thought or belief on one side of a three-by-five index card. On the other side, write several counterstatements. Carry one or more different cards with you each day so that you can review these and practice. The cards can remind you of the need to pay attention to your thoughts and actively work at countering them.

Focus on Positive Thoughts. Make sure you do not focus solely on negative thoughts. Each day, pay attention to your accomplishments, progress, and positive thoughts. Some people find it helpful to keep track of the actual numbers of negative and positive thoughts. The idea is not only to track numbers and types of thoughts but also to chart changes that occur over time. For example, if you note that your negative thoughts are gradually decreasing and your positive thoughts are increasing, you will feel a sense of progress and accomplishment, even if you still are bothered by negative thoughts some of the time.

Make a List of Your Accomplishments. Write out a list of your accomplishments, no matter how small they may seem. Some people find it helpful to take periodic inventory of their accomplishments. This may help you keep things in better perspective, since it is so easy to downplay the many things that you accomplish. Acknowledge your success! You can also share your list with another person.

Make a List of Your Positive Traits. Write out a list of your positive personality traits. Focus on your strengths and the aspects of your personality that you or other people like. The self-help programs advocate taking a personal inventory to help identify positive (and negative) traits. The idea is to build on the positives and work on changing the negatives.

Use Self-Praise. Compliment yourself when you make progress, take a risk, achieve a goal, or do good work. Even if you make a mistake or fail at something, you can praise yourself for taking a risk and trying. Remember, efforts can be praised, not just results! We usually compliment others much more quickly than ourselves. You are not an egotistical person just because you give yourself some praise now and then.

Remember the Pain of Addiction. Review the negative things that happened as a result of your addiction. Always keep in mind the negative effects of addiction on your physical, mental, social, or spiritual health. Remember what your addiction has done to others as well, such as your family. This can help you avoid the tunnel vision that often comes after you have been in recovery for a while.

Remember the Benefits of Recovery. Review the benefits of recovery. What have you gained so far from being in recovery? What other benefits will come to you in the future as your recovery progresses? Weigh the benefits of recovery against the pain of addiction.

Use humor. Some people find they can change how they think by injecting humor into the situation. Humor can help you see how absurd your thinking is. Exaggerate your distorted thinking and take it to an absurd extreme. Or poke fun at yourself for thinking in such a distorted way.

Use the Serenity Prayer. One of the many tools of the self-help programs is the serenity prayer. Repeating it out loud and reflecting on it can help. It goes like this: "God grant me the serenity to accept the things I cannot change, the courage to change the things I can, and the wisdom to know the difference." It is a very simple prayer, yet it carries a powerful message.

Repeat the Slogans of the Self-Help Programs. The self-help programs have a number of slogans that aim to combat addictive or "stinking" thinking. Some of the more commonly used ones are: "One day at a time." "This too will pass." "Think before you drink (take drugs, overeat, gamble, have sex]." and "Fake it [recovery] until you make it."

Use Thought Interruption. Try to catch yourself when you are thinking too negatively. Tell yourself, "stop it." Challenge yourself as to why you are thinking so negatively.

Use the A–B–C Method. Dr. Albert Ellis developed "rational emotive therapy," an approach that helps people learn to think differently about themselves and their difficulties. Many people assume that events cause emotional reactions. Dr. Ellis's approach assumes that your self-talk or beliefs about the events determine the emotional consequences. He suggests following the A–B–C method to help you change your viewpoints.

The first step in the A–B–C method is to identify the events that activate your feelings (A). The next step is to identify your beliefs or self-talk about these events (B). Next identify the emotional consequences of your thinking and paying attention to how strong your feelings are (C).

For example, your boss criticizes you for a mistake you made. You are very likely to feel upset; however, being mildly upset is different from being extremely upset. There are different degrees of reaction. During the process of identifying your A–B–Cs, you can challenge or dispute the irrational beliefs that lead to your uncomfortable feelings. The following cases are two examples.

Example 1

A—*activating event:* Diana gets a call from an old friend with whom she used to get high. Her friend suggests they get together because he has some dynamite coke.

B—*belief or thought:* She thinks, "I'd love to get high just once, then let the stuff alone. I've been in recovery for a long time, I really deserve a reward."

C—*consequence:* At first, Diana feels a great deal of excitement. Then she feels anxious and a bit guilty.

Counterstatements: She could counter her thoughts about getting high and deserving a reward with statements like these:

1. Sure, I'd love to get high. But I'm not going to do it. It won't do anything but mess me up anyway.

2. Yeah, yeah, I miss the high sometimes. Big deal. I'll get over it. I don't miss the trouble that came with my addiction.

3. So I'm thinking about rewarding myself with coke. What a con job. You know what they say, you can't con another con. I'm hip to my own cons. I just won't cop any more dope. No if's, and's, or but's about it!

Example 2

A—activating event: Sam turns in a written report to his boss, who returns it a few days later with a lot of corrections made in red ink.

B—belief: He thinks it is terrible that his boss did not like his report, he wonders if he is incompetent, and he believes his boss dislikes him.

C—consequence: Sam feels anxious and upset.

Counterstatements: He could dispute his self-defeating thoughts (B) by countering with statements like these:

1. My boss made a lot of changes. Next time I'll make sure I know what he wants in the report before I write it.

2. The boss is tough, but he makes a lot of good suggestions. I've learned something from his critical comments and can use it in the future.

3. Everyone in the office gets corrections from the boss, so it's really nothing personal. He's very particular, but usually correct in his suggestions or criticisms.

4. I'm not incompetent just because my boss made a bunch of corrections on my report. There are a lot of things I do very well. It's not fair to judge myself based only on one report.

The way you think has a great deal of impact on how you feel and act. All aspects of your life are affected by the beliefs you hold. No one approach will work the same for everyone in changing the way people think; find the techniques that work the best for you and use them. I recommend that you have a variety of techniques or approaches to rely on so that if one does not work in a given situation you can try another. Keep in mind that you won't know what's best for you until you try the different approaches.

7

Changing Personality Traits and Character Defects

Y OUR personality traits are your patterns of viewing and relating to the world and yourself. These personality traits show in your attitudes and behaviors and in your relationships with other people. They play a very big role in your recovery as well as in your overall happiness in life. When someone refers to you as a certain type of person—selfish, aggressive, sensitive, loving, responsible, dependent—they are talking about your traits.

Both professional and self-help recovery programs put a great deal of emphasis on the need to change personality traits, particularly the ones that cause difficulty in your life. In fact, two of the steps of the twelve-step recovery programs emphasize the importance of taking a personal inventory. Step four states that we "made a searching and fearless moral inventory of ourselves." This inventory involves taking a look at many personal aspects of yourself, including your personality traits. The idea is to build on strengths and correct defects. Step ten states that we "continued to take personal inventory and when we were wrong promptly admitted it." This implies that changing your traits is an ongoing process and that it is important to make corrections when you do something wrong or make mistakes with others. Developing new traits is sometimes just as important as correcting problematic ones.

When a specific trait causes some type of problem for you or others, it is sometimes called a character "defect." The term implies that something is wrong or defective with a pattern of behavior and needs to be changed. Everyone has defects of character, whether or not they have addictive disorders. However, working on changing character is a common area of focus in recovery from an addiction.

Whether a given character trait came before or after your addiction is open to debate. The reality is that some traits probably contributed to your addiction while others resulted from it. Whatever the cause, your recovery will be enhanced when you are willing to examine your traits and change those that create problems in your life or cause you personal distress or feelings of discomfort.

Every single person has positive and negative personality traits. If you look closely enough, you will find traits that would make your life better if you changed them. However, it is not always easy to see which traits you need to change; you may only see one side of the coin and believe that a certain trait is beneficial when, in reality, it creates problems for you.

Personality Disorders and Traits

DISORDERS

Sometimes, a set of personality traits can be part of what experts call a "personality disorder." Having a personality disorder is more serious than having some character defects. A "disorder" implies a disturbance in your personality that negatively affects your life or well-being. The following list gives a few examples of how specific traits may be part of a possible personality disorder.

It is one thing to be somewhat mistrustful and cautious with other people; it is entirely another matter, however, if you are extremely suspicious of others without just cause, or do not develop any relationships with other people as a result.

It is one thing to be sensitive to criticism from others; but it is entirely another matter to be so hypersensitive and worried about criticism that you totally avoid relationships or only enter into those in which you are guaranteed unconditional acceptance.

It is one thing to be passive and dependent on others; it is entirely another matter when you let others make all of your decisions and totally rely on them to meet your needs or to define yourself.

It is one thing to be dishonest and occasionally lie or distort the truth; it is quite another to be a pathological liar who cannot be trusted and who always distorts the truth for personal gain.

There are thirteen different types of personality disorders. Each type has its own particular cluster of symptoms or behaviors. However, many of these disorders have the following general characteristics in common:

they are inflexible and not easily changed,

they are maladaptive,

they create problems in your life (job, school, relationships, and so on), and

they cause personal suffering or distress.

Not everyone with an addiction has a personality disorder. However, according to many research studies, personality disorders are often associated with addictions. Disorders often need to be addressed as part of recovery. Failure to do so could make you more vulnerable to relapse.

Even if you do not have a personality disorder, you may have some related traits. In fact, it is not unusual for a person to have traits associated with several different types of personality disorders. The important point to keep in mind is that you have the option of changing your character traits.

TRAITS

Do not view your individual personality traits as either totally healthy or unhealthy. At times a trait usually viewed as negative can be used positively. For example, Curtis is a regional supervisor for about twenty-five sales consultants. He is viewed as an aggressive "go-getter," and his aggressiveness was a major factor in his success as a sales consultant as well as in his subsequent promotion. Curtis speaks his mind forthrightly, even at the expense of hurting other peoples' feelings. Curtis sometimes upsets people with his aggressive talk and behavior. On the other hand, he also uses his aggressiveness to help his sales staff in various ways. When he feels that management has made a decision that is unfair to his staff, he will argue until his position is heard and considered. As a result, he was able to get several decisions reversed, to the benefit of his staff. Curtis's aggressive pressure on his staff has pushed them to increase their sales. Even though his pushy nature bothers some sales consultants at times, they see that it has influenced their productivity.

On the other hand, sometimes a "positive" trait can cause personal harm and suffering. Consider Melissa, for instance. She is a kind, loving, and giving person. Many people come to her for advice and solace in times of difficulty. She is always there to listen to those who need her help. Melissa has helped quite a few people over the years and is seen as someone to lean on or get advice from.

However, her kind and helpful nature has led to problems. Melissa has trouble setting limits and saying no to people when she does not have the time, energy, or interest to help. So when she reluctantly helps someone, she sometimes harbors resentment inside. Melissa will still help friends when she feels resentful, and others have no idea of her feelings about helping them. "And," she says, "when I let a lot of resentment build up, I'm much more prone to reward or nurture myself with food. The only problem is, I often go on an eating binge. In a crazy way, I rationalize that this is OK, that I deserve it for what I've given to others."

In addition, her husband Brad gets angry with her because he feels slighted. Brad says, "She's always so busy helping others that she doesn't seem to have much time for me. The constant phone calls from her friends requesting help or support are an inconvenience. We often get interrupted during dinner. It's really hard to spend an hour alone without the damn phone ringing."

This case clearly illustrates how Melissa's positive traits of kindness and helpfulness are a great help to others. Yet they cause conflicts for her and for her marriage. Emotional reactions associated with these traits can contribute to a relapse as well. In

Melissa's case, she went on eating binges as a way of dealing with her built-up resentments or her perceived need to have a reward.

Common Personality Traits

Usually, your personality traits have a combination of positive and negative effects on you and your relationships. Keep in mind that the following discussion and examples portray particular traits developed to such a degree that they cause problems. However, at times supposedly negative traits like self-centeredness are adaptive and necessary, and problems do not occur as a result. But, if you are self-centered all or most of the time, this trait is likely to cause serious problems in your life.

In the sections that follow, a number of specific personality traits are discussed. The experiences of recovering individuals are presented to show how their traits affected their lives and how they changed them. Because it is impossible to discuss all of the various personality traits, I focus on the ones that appear most commonly among people with addictive disorders. Nevertheless, any personality trait, however obscure, can contribute to your recovery or be a factor in relapse.

In some instances, I discuss opposite traits to show both sides of the coin (for example, passive and aggressive, self-centered and other-centered). The ideal is to strike a balance and to be able to adapt various aspects of your personality to the situation at hand.

The traits discussed are ones that many people can relate to, not just those with an addictive disease or habit. Make a note of the traits you most identify with and the ones you need to work on changing. While some ideas are presented on how to change particular traits, you will also need to explore your own ways of changing as well. What helps one person change may not work for another.

INHIBITED

If you are very closed, or inhibited, you probably have a lot of trouble talking and sharing with others. As a result, others do not get a chance to know what you think, how you feel, what your interests or abilities are, or other things about you. Being inhibited can involve you in one-sided relationships and interfere with your opportunities to get close to or intimate with others.

If you are too inhibited, you may not feel comfortable participating in support group meetings where important issues about addiction and recovery are shared and discussed. Holding on to your personal issues or struggles can then backfire and contribute to a relapse. One of the most effective ways of dealing with such personal conflicts is to share them with others. When you repress them, anxiety and tension are more likely to build up.

Gene, who has been recovering for several years from compulsive gambling, told how he slowly learned to open up in his relationships with others. "I had a lot of acquaintances, but no real friends, if you know what I mean. When I was gambling, I would talk with the best of them because I knew so much. But when it came to other things in life, or talking about who I really was, or what I felt, I just couldn't do it. I was a closed book in this regard. Very inhibited you could say.

"Change took me quite a while. I did it in small steps. I'd let one person know some personal things about me. The more I trusted, the more I eventually shared about my inner self. Then, it became easier to let others know about me. I found that other people still liked me even if I told them about some of the rotten things I had done in my gambling, or things about myself I didn't like.

"Eventually, I began talking more at GA meetings. I started out sharing what I thought were safe details about myself. In time, I could be more honest and open. I stopped being closed and let other people in my life. And, you know what? I found out that when you stop being so inhibited and begin to share, you feel better about yourself. You get closer to others, too, It takes some time and a lot of effort, but it can be done."

UNINHIBITED

On the other hand, you can be too expressive and open—or, uninhibited. You can share too much about yourself and overwhelm other people. You may say whatever you think or feel, without regard for how the other person will receive it. This kind of openness can push other people away. The ideal is to strike a balance between being too open and expressive and not being open and expressive at all.

Lisa told how she worked on this trait as part of her ongoing recovery from compulsive sexual behaviors. "I used to talk to anybody about anything. My thoughts, feelings, and actions were an open book to the world. Like, I would go to a beauty parlor and lay out my whole life, even if this was the first time there. I would even share personal details about my relationships, my feelings, and my views on sex without thinking about who might hear me.

"My openness about my sexual preferences and behaviors was often a stimulus for others to open up. It was a cue for them to talk and perhaps even to take things a step further. Even people I just had met or barely knew would be exposed to my open views about sex. It was one of the ways I seduced men to satisfy my compulsive sexual needs. Not all men liked this, mind you. Some got anxious or turned off.

"In recovery, I learned to be more discreet about what personal things I shared and with whom I shared them. I made a conscious effort not to open up all at once, especially to people I just met. So, I slowed down and stopped routinely sharing so many details of my private life without thinking about how this affected others. I also had to stop discussing my views and experiences about sex with men because it gave them the message that I was interested in them. Plus, the more I got going talking about sex with a man, the more prone I was to relapsing and giving in to my sexual impulses.

"It wasn't just sex, however. I had to learn to put the brakes on talking about other things too openly. Like my divorce, problems with my parents, and feeling lonely. It finally dawned on me that people who didn't know me all that well weren't sure how to take it if I expressed these personal things."

SELF-CENTEREDNESS

This trait is characterized by a tendency to view things primarily from one point of view: your own. Everything revolves around you—your needs, wants, ideas, problems, achievements, and experiences.

You may show little regard or interest toward others and talk or do only what is important to you. This leads to placing undue demands on others to cater to your needs. In some cases, if you are a self-centered person you require constant attention from others much of the time and place unrealistic value on things said or done. It is as though everyone has to be interested in what you do and what you think or feel. You see yourself as very important and make everything in your life one-sided. There is little, if any, mutuality when you are too self-centered.

John, for example, always planned his family's vacations around activities that were important to him. It never dawned on him to ask his wife or children what they wanted to do. On a day-to-day level, he always talked about his work and activities. "How are you?" or "How was your day?" were foreign expressions to John. If someone talked about an important issue or experience, John was quick to change the subject to his own experience. He was so self-centered that he never realized people could not stand this behavior and often avoided him.

Consider John's description of how he began to change his self-centeredness following some heart-to-heart talks with his Alcoholics Anonymous sponsor and his family. "When my AA sponsor first pointed out to me that the only person I ever seemed to focus on was myself, I thought, "What does this SOB know about me anyway?' But you see, my reaction was just another example of my self-centeredness. I guess what really bothered me was that my sponsor told me what my wife had been telling me for years. I could blow her off and believe whatever the hell I wanted to. With my AA sponsor though, it was different. I knew that to stay sober, I had to pay attention to him. And, it forced me to be more open with my wife. In fact, he told me that I needed to discuss this character defect with my family to learn how they saw things.

"So, on his advice, I initiated a discussion with my wife and kids. To make a long story short, they told me they really felt good about how good I was doing staying sober. I'd been sober for over a year. But, every one of them said that all I ever talk about is myself and I never give the impression of being interested in what they are doing.

"I'll tell you what really put this in focus. My oldest son, a college student, said, 'Dad, you don't even know what the hell

I'm studying. In fact, I bet you don't even know what year I'm in, do you?' The truth of the matter was, I didn't know what he was studying or what year he was in. My daughter put the icing on the cake when she said there were many times that she excused herself from the dinner table as quickly as possible just so she could get away from my constant chatter about myself or my endless stream of stories.

"I won't lie to you, it hasn't been easy to change my self-centered nature. I've had to change some of my beliefs and attitudes, such as what happens with me is the most important thing in the family or that my family has to know all the details of my experiences. What I've been working on the most is simply letting others talk without feeling like I always have to cut them off and add my two cents. And, if you can believe this, I'm learning how to have a mutual conversation by asking questions about other people. A couple times a month, I call my son and spend most of the conversation asking him about his school activities and really listening to him.

"At home, I make it a point to let my wife and daughter talk about things they are doing, or how they think and feel about certain issues. We've even agreed that if I ramble on with my long-winded stories that really can get boring, they can let me know. It's all worth it because they aren't irritated with me like they used to be and we are actually having better family discussions. I'm doing better at this change with my kids than my wife and I have some more work to do. But things have improved since I started changing this trait."

OTHER-CENTEREDNESS

You can be too focused on other people as well. You may put too much energy and emphasis on catering to or thinking about other people. You pay much more attention to them and their needs than your own. This can lead to excessive worry about others' opinions of you or to unrealistic attempts to please others constantly. Your decisions may be based more on what you perceive others to need than what you need. Your needs take a back seat.

On the surface, this trait is less problematic than self-centeredness because other people like you to focus on them and pay attention to their needs. Yet keep in mind that you can harbor resentments or other negative feelings or have problematic relationships if you always focus on others and not yourself. You probably tie your self-esteem to what you believe others think about you. You give your needs and interests a low priority.

Barbara, who is recovering from drug addiction, told her story about being too other-centered. "It started way back when I was a kid. My mom seemed to be always worried about what this or that person thought or liked. It didn't matter what the issue was, whether it was how we dressed, talked, acted, or even how the house looked. She just always obsessed about other people. It was especially true related to my father. God, she drove us nuts with trying to make sure we constantly did things to please him. You know, in all the years we went on family vacations, we never once went where mom wanted to go.

"Wouldn't you know, lucky old me seemed to inherit this trait. I was one of those people that others liked because I listened so well. But I compromised myself because I always gave in and made sure I did what others wanted. Even with things as simple as which movie to go to. I did what everyone else wanted, not what I wanted to do.

"When I first started to take care of myself and focus on my own needs, I felt guilty. It was like this was wrong to do. It wasn't just the behavior that I had to change, but my attitudes and beliefs as well. I had to really, truly believe that it wasn't wrong to focus on me and not always attend to the needs of others. But once I accepted that it was actually better for everyone not to be so other-centered, and in fact it was even OK at times to be self-centered, it was a lot easier.

"Now I'm able to make decisions and do things that I want to do. I'm still able to focus on others, but there's a better balance now in my life. I find I feel better about myself as a result, and don't get taken advantage of as much."

PASSIVENESS

If you are too passive, you more than likely take a reactive rather than a proactive stance toward things. With this trait, you let things happen and give power and control to other people. They make decisions for you. As a result, your rights, feelings, opinions, and needs are ignored or minimized. You feel taken advantage of and probably even blame others when the problem is not how they treat you but how you let them treat you. You allow your well-being and happiness to be controlled by others.

You tend to keep your opinions, thoughts, or feelings to yourself. You may act in a timid or shy fashion. People can walk on you and take advantage of you, and can even be unaware of it. You may feel upset or even be steaming on the inside, but no one else knows because you act as though everything is just fine. At the extreme, you may present yourself as being helpless and totally dependent upon others. Since you do not want to rock the boat, you keep your thoughts and feelings to yourself.

Ron is a hard-working, competent accountant. At work, he had trouble standing up to his boss if he was criticized about something his boss thought he did incorrectly. Colleagues dumped work on him many times, but Ron passively accepted this, even though it irritated him a great deal. His wife was bossy, demanding, and controlling; but at home, like at work, Ron passively accepted this situation as his fate and usually gave in to his wife. Deep down, however, he felt resentful.

You can show your passivity in an aggressive way (called passive-aggressive behavior). This means that you indirectly express yourself. For example, Ron seldom said anything directly to his wife when he was upset. Instead, he would sometimes "forget" important dates, such as his wife's birthday or their anniversary. Or he would "forget" to call her when he was going to arrive home late from work so that she wondered if anything had happened to him.

One of the most common passive-aggressive behaviors is the "silent treatment." Even if verbally you deny that anything is wrong, you know deep inside that you are angry or upset with another person. You show it by not talking much—perhaps not at all. In some cases, you avoid people you feel upset with. In work situations, this anger may show in "losing" papers, missing meetings, or not completing specific work assignments.

Ron shared a little about how he worked on changing his passivity. "It was simple what I had to do—learn to assert myself and stop being a doormat and a wimp! What was less simple was actually doing things differently. Truthfully, it took a lot of planning, practicing, and making mistakes. But guess what?

Things do get better when you stop being passive and speak up for yourself.

"I started changing this trait at home with my wife. While I still did many of the things she asked me to do, I became more honest and open, letting her know when I was upset about something. She was quite surprised at first. Actually, she didn't realize how much her bossiness really bothered me because I never said anything about it before this time. My wife didn't make a big personality change, mind you, because her nature is to be controlling and bossy. But she toned down enough that I was much less irritated with her. Oh, I still have to remind her from time to time to lay off me, but overall it's worked out pretty good. And, by the way, I haven't forgotten any important dates in the past year.

"Change at work came easier with my colleagues than my boss. After convincing myself that my rights and needs were important, I started telling them no, and refused to do certain jobs that I thought were being dumped on me. They showed greater respect to me as a result and began approaching me differently. It took longer to feel comfortable not being so passive with my boss. At first, I started by giving my opinions in situations where he differed with me. Before this, I always just accepted what he had to say without giving my view of the situation. In time, I even learned to disagree with him. Probably the biggest change was taking the bull by the horns and initiating discussions with my boss on problem areas that I anticipated. In the past my pattern was to wait for him to find the problem and approach me. Now, I'm more proactive and assertive in this regard."

AGGRESSIVENESS

The flip side of passivity is aggressiveness. If you are too aggressive, you ignore the rights, opinions, needs, or feelings of others. You may be very forceful in expressing yourself to others. At the extreme, you are like a bull in a china shop who plunges ahead to get what you want or need. No one or nothing can stop you. You are bossy and demanding, often violating the rights of others.

You can be abrupt or abrasive if you are very aggressive. You may blurt out what you think or feel with no regard for how others may be affected. You speak your mind and do your own thing. In some instances, you can show aggressiveness in the form of hostility or overt anger. You may intimidate others and push them away.

Don, a compulsive overeater and alcoholic, shared his story about toning down his aggressiveness. "My nature is to be loud and aggressive. Been this way most of my life. When I was drinking, I'd really get into heated arguments. I was ready to fight at the drop of a pin. Booze unleashed me, so to speak. Even when I didn't drink, though, I would lash out at others and create arguments over about anything.

"But this brought me nothing but trouble. I mean, c'mon, I'm a grown man with a wife and children. So I had to stop being a bully and mouthing off at others. And stop picking fights. It certainly was easier when I wasn't loaded up on booze.

"I also cut down on yelling at the kids. Used to scare the hell out of them sometimes. Now, I ain't cut down yelling totally, mind you, but quite a bit. And, I stopped bossing my wife around so much. I started asking for things from her instead of demanding them like I did in the past. Even learned to respect her opinion about things.

"I don't speak my mind so freely anymore, either. Like I said, I used to fly off at the mouth. Didn't care who heard me, if I had an opinion or feeling, I'd blurt it out. I realized you can't always do this, that there are times where you gotta keep your trap shut.

"A couple times a week, I stop off at the gym. Swim and lift some weights. It's been a great way to let off tension. I can direct my aggression toward exercise. It helps, that's for sure."

CONTROLLING

If you are controlling, you feel a need to be in control of most, if not all, situations or interactions with other people. You have to be the one who determines the outcome of a given situation. You can be controlling in a very direct and forthright way, or your need to control can be passively expressed and less visible to others. You may, for example, drag your feet if you feel like you have to give in to another person's decision.

If you have a great need always to be in control, it is highly likely that you are rigid, compulsive, and/or perfectionist. Being rigid makes it difficult to compromise or bend for others. You see your way as the right way in all situations. If you are not in control, you feel anxious and uncertain.

Your need to control shows itself in a variety of circumstances—the major as well as the minor situations or decisions in life. If your need for control is great, there's a good chance that you will not be open to others' suggestions about your recovery. You will probably prefer doing it your way, even if your way has not been very successful.

One of the big problems of controlling behavior is that it pushes people away. Others feel they cannot get anywhere with you if they perceive you as a person who has to have everything your way. They think, "Why should I bother?"

Brenda, who is recovering from compulsive gambling, shared her journey to change her trait of being controlling. "I guess I learned at a very young age that if I didn't take charge and grab control, things just wouldn't get done at home. My mother was drunk a lot and my father seldom was home. As the oldest of five, I felt it was up to me to protect my brothers and sisters and make them feel that someone was in control.

"In looking back, I can see that other kids were drawn to me because I was a leader. But I can also see that some kids avoided me because things always had to be my way. I still remember vividly my first boyfriend throwing up his hands in disgust and telling me he was tired of everything always having to be my way.

"I married a passive type of guy, probably because it was easy to control him. He shocked me one day, though, when he blurted out how tired he was of my treating him like a kid. I used to give him a list of things to do around the house. To top it off, I also told him what to do first and how he should do certain tasks on the list. You'll probably think I'm a bit wacky, but I also picked out his clothes for work. You could probably guess which of us made the decisions on things to buy for the house, where to go on vacation, and where to go out for dinner. I'm embarrassed to say this, but even if the family sat down in the evening to play a game for fun, I had to be the one who decided what we would play, and I made sure we played it the 'correct' way.

"When I quit gambling, I was so depressed and upset that I saw a psychiatrist in addition to going to GA meetings. My doctor was great. She helped me see just how much of a problem my need to control was and where it all apparently started. I had to learn to change some of my very deeply ingrained beliefs, such as 'things got done right only if I did them' and 'to be competent and effective I always had to be in control.'

"Then, I had to gradually let others make decisions and give input so that my behaviors changed. There were times in which I asked my husband and kids to make certain decisions without my input. I can't tell you how hard it was at first to resist the impulse to give my two cents' worth. And, I stopped giving my husband 'to do' lists.

"At work, I also made conscious efforts to not make all decisions and orchestrate things so I was always in control. I stopped insisting things be done my way all of the time, even if I disagreed with one of my office staff.

"I won't lie to you. I've done much better, but I'm not always comfortable giving up control, and I have to work really hard at it. But I know it's better for everyone."

IMPULSIVENESS

Many relapses occur when people act on an impulse to engage in their addictive behavior. Or they may act on impulse and do something that contributes to a relapse. Ron, a cocaine addict and alcoholic, was invited by a friend to join a group of people flying to Las Vegas the next day for a weekend of gambling and entertainment. Even though Ron knew this was a wild, partying crowd he gave in to his impulse to go. He thought to himself, "I don't have to drink. Besides, I could use a change of scenery." Ron lasted about four hours in the casino before he took a drink. It wasn't long before he drank a few more. After alcohol had lowered his control, he snorted several lines of cocaine as well.

If you frequently are impulsive, you tend to act before you think rather than the reverse. You do what you want, when you want to, with whomever you want, without giving much consideration to the possible consequences of your behavior for yourself or others in your life.

This trait shows up both verbally (in what you say) as well as nonverbally (in what you do or how you behave). You may blurt out what you think or feel to another person, even if it is inappropriate to do so. Mike shared these examples of impulsive statements he had made to others. "I told my boss that he was full of shit during a discussion of a matter where we had differing opinions. He's not the kind of guy that takes too kindly to this kind of statement.

"When out on a first date with a woman I really liked and was attracted to, I told her how much I was attracted to her and wanted to make love with her. This made her feel uncomfortable and she refused to go out with me again.

Impulsiveness can show in a wide range of behaviors related to your addiction as well as in any area of your life. Some examples from several recovering people are given below.

- "I quit my job because I was pissed at my boss and tired of him always getting on my case. I didn't even have another job to go to or much money saved to help me get by until I found another job. And, I'm supposed to get married pretty soon." —Al, age 24.

- "My wife and I went shopping to get her a new pair of tennis shoes. Well, we spent over two hundred dollars on clothes she didn't really need. Then, we stopped at a furniture store and spent about two thousand dollars on new furniture. This all happened quickly and during a time in which we were supposed to stop charging things. We impulsively spent money we didn't have." —Dennis, age 41.

- "I fell for this guy I met through a friend. We saw each other about ten times in about two weeks, then I let him move in with me. He was wild and fun to be with. Problem is, when I went away with him on a whim, I relapsed and got high with him. He got tired or bored with me a couple of months later and moved out. Oh, I'll get over it, but David, my four-year-old, was really taking to him." —Liz, age 29.

- "My wife asked me to stop and pick up a few things from the store on the way home from work. I went to one of those convenience stores and bought two nude magazines. Later that night when everyone was in bed, I read these and masturbated a couple of times. The next day I called some old female friends and arranged to meet one of them. I had refrained from pornography and affairs for almost a year. Now here I was, on my way back to my sexual addiction." —Lance, age 35.

- "I got upset at my husband following an argument over the bills. He made me feel guilty for the financial crunch we were going through. So I thought, "the hell with him" and got in my car. I drove straight to the bakery. I knocked off a half-dozen doughnuts and some cookies, then stopped somewhere else for ice cream. Binging always calmed me down when I was upset . . . at least at first. Before I got home, I made myself throw up so I wouldn't gain weight from all of the calories. —Rebecca, age 31.

Being impulsive on occasion can add a sense of fun or spontaneity to life and is not bad—unless, of course, you act on impulse in relation to your addiction.

However, if you are commonly impulsive, you are in trouble if you do not recognize and change this trait. Impulsiveness leads to making poor decisions in your life because you do what you want instead of what is best for you. You think about immediate or short-term pleasure or gain rather than about long-term consequences. And you seldom if ever think much about the impact of your impulsive behavior on others.

Consider how Helen, a woman recovering from compulsive sexual behaviors, worked on changing her impulsiveness. "They say live one day at a time. Well, I had been doing that all along, but not the way it was intended. I just did whatever the hell I wanted. I was deep in debt because I ran up a bunch of charge cards to their limit, buying things on impulse, not things I really needed or could afford. My mother was upset with me because I kept dumping my four-year-old on her without giving her any notice or even asking her if she'd watch him. And, I kept getting hooked up with guys who were losers. It wasn't unusual to be seeing a couple guys at the same time. Even if I lived with a man, I'd get involved with others. None of my relationships last more than a few months.

"I started changing my relationship pattern because this was not only hurting me but my son as well. To change, I first had to look at why I'd let men move in my apartment after knowing them just a few weeks. This process helped me discover that I confused sexual attraction and attention with love. It also helped me see my sick attitude about needing to own a man where there was mutual attraction. Along with this attitude change, I made a commitment to not let anyone move in with me and my son unless I were certain a long-term relationship was likely to happen. Since I was fairly new to recovery, I took the advice of others in recovery and made a commitment to give myself at least a half year or so before even letting myself think about an involved relationship. I also made an agreement to discuss any attractions that I felt toward a man with someone I trust. Just to get an objective ear.

"Believe it or not, not spending money impulsively was harder to change. I cut up all of my charge cards except one. I made a commitment to pay them off one at a time, and to limit the amount of charges on the one card I kept. In reviewing my spending behavior, I discovered a high-risk situation was going to the mall—for any reason! Even if I went to the mall only to buy my son an ice-cream cone, I bought other things. Very seldom did I pay cash. So, out went the credit cards. And my mall trips were very few and far between."

IRRESPONSIBILITY

If you are irresponsible, you avoid living up to your responsibilities. You may not get things done on time, not care much about the consequences of your actions, or go about life in a rather haphazard fashion.

This trait is likely to show in your behavior in a variety of different situations: in your family and social relationships, at work or school, and in how you conduct your affairs in life. It will cause you not to meet your obligations in life. Perhaps you do not pay your bills on time, pay attention to the needs of your children or spouse, or follow through with commitments at work, school, or in your social relationships. Or maybe you do not do things that you are supposed to do, or you do things that show poor judgment.

If you are an irresponsible person, it is very likely that many problems have resulted from this. You cannot be depended upon. You upset other people with your actions. You blame others for your problems and difficulties and find it hard to accept responsibility. And you probably do not often consider the future. Instead, you focus on the present and on what you want or need right now.

Look now at how David went about changing his irresponsible ways. "One of the best things that ever happened to me was going to jail. I got arrested a couple of times. The last time I got busted though, I got sent away for a couple of years. My first couple of months in the joint, I still blamed others for my problems. 'They' put me there, not me!

"Since I was a drug addict they put heat on me to go to this program. After a while though, I quit kidding myself and started to see the seriousness of my addiction. When I later reviewed my life in great detail, it was clear that my life was doing my own thing. Money, relationships, work, my apartment, you name it, I just wasn't responsible. Except for making my car payments on time and keeping it in good condition.

"My old man told me I'd never amount to anything if I didn't clean up my act. Man, was he ever right. I guess my turnaround started when I accepted responsibility for my circumstances. Nobody but me put me in jail. I was to blame, not anybody else.

"Before I got out, I had some long talks with my old man. Apologized for the shit I done to him. He agreed to help get me back on my feet and let me live at home for a while. But there were some conditions. Like getting a job, paying rent, and going to NA meetings.

"As my recovery progressed, I settled down more and more. Paid my bills on time. Didn't miss no work unless I was really sick. Did what I was supposed to do in the family. When I moved out to my own place, I made sure I visited home a lot. Started doin' stuff I'd never done before like giving them cards and presents for mother's and father's days and their birthdays. My old man even told me once how proud he was of me, for turning things around."

OVERRESPONSIBILITY

Although usually less problematic than its opposite discussed above, overresponsibility—being overly responsible—can cause you problems as well. The problems can be quite serious and can create a good deal of conflict or personal distress as well as difficulties in your relationships.

With this trait, you are too focused on making sure that things get done and that other people's needs are satisfied. You are too sensitive to others and not sensitive enough to your own needs. In addition, your sense of importance gets exaggerated. After all, someone as responsible as you are must be quite important.

Like any other trait, this one may show at work or school, in your relationships with family or friends, or in virtually any other area of your life. You may get too involved in solving the problems of friends or family members. In fact, this trait can contribute to intruding into the lives of others. You can inhibit others' growth by being too responsible. For example, Marcy was very quick to intervene when one of her children was having a problem with other children at school. She felt she had to get things settled quickly and told her children exactly what they should do. The problem was twofold: first, her instructions to her children often did not work or caused additional problems; and, second, her behavior reinforced her childrens' inability to solve their own problems. On some level, they knew that their mother would do things for them and depended too much on her.

At work, Marcy felt responsible for the happiness of her staff. As a supervisor who assigned work and managed a clinic, she tried very hard to please other people. As a result, if someone else was upset, her first reaction was either to feel somehow responsible for their dissatisfaction or to feel responsible for making the situation better. Because Marcy was such an over-responsible person, she had trouble delegating assignments and overwhelmed herself by doing too much of the work. And, she was prone to feeling guilty and inadequate if work fell behind.

Marcy also worried about running the household and taking care of her husband's needs. Despite being a very busy professional woman and the mother of two children, she took it upon herself to run the family. Although her husband was cooperative and helpful, Marcy felt that her job was to keep everything running smoothly at home. If people were not happy, then she thought it must be her fault.

In her friendships, Marcy often overextended herself. She had trouble saying no and often gave what little free time she had to others. This was often done out of her excessive sense of responsibility.

Her one escape from all of these burdens was food. It was one sure way of nurturing herself and giving something to herself to compensate for all that she had done for others. Unfortunately, Marcy was quite overweight and prone to compulsive overeating binges.

She finally joined Overeaters Anonymous and started a program for recovery from compulsive overeating. After completing her personal inventory with her sponsor, Marcy knew she had her work cut out for her. She knew her sense of overresponsibility had to be toned down considerably. Listen to her journey of change. "There was so much involved in changing, it's hard to know where to begin. I had to do things a lot differently. At first, it was hard. I felt awkward. And, to be honest, I think others would prefer me the old way, when I took care of them.

"Now, mind you, I had trouble with this whole idea. It seemed so out of place to not feel responsible for everything around me. My sponsor told me to change my behaviors and not to worry about how I thought about this stuff. My attitudes would change later.

"Well, I started by making a list of all the things I was doing for my husband and kids. I picked a few things and agreed to stop taking responsibility for these. Like doing a lot of my husband's errands. I mean, after all, we both work. So I told him I couldn't be doing a lot of these things, that it was wearing me out. I also asked him to help more at home. He agreed to help more with grocery shopping and laundry. I know this doesn't sound like a big deal, but it saved me a lot of time. I also told my kids I'd stop cleaning up their rooms and the messes they made. In fact, my husband and I made a little chart listing chores and responsibilities of the kids. I'll tell you what. It felt strange at first because if I saw a mess at home, my impulse was to clean it up.

"Gradually, I learned to relax more when we had friends over to the house. In the past, I was so worried about everyone having a good time that I constantly was checking to see if they needed anything. So, I learned to sit and socialize instead. If they had a good time that was fine. If they didn't, well I could no longer burden myself with feeling so doggone responsible.

"I changed some things at work, too. Delegated more work so others got more involved. And guess what? Things got done.

"Probably the biggest change was taking better care of myself. Focusing on my needs and making me feel good. When you feel responsible for others all the time, you neglect yourself. So I'm working hard at not neglecting me. I even joined an aerobics class and go a couple times a week. This not only helps my physical health but my mental well-being as well."

PERFECTIONISM

Over and over again, people with addictions talk about feeling burdened by perfectionism. This trait causes you to be rigid. You have high expectations and are easily frustrated because life is quite imperfect in so many ways. When you get down to it, it is impossible to achieve perfection in most things in life; but, by expecting it, you set yourself up to feel bad.

Perfectionism can also be applied to other people in your life. But others certainly cannot meet your standards for perfection. So you criticize them, if not to their faces at least to yourself. You are quick to see their mistakes, faults, defects, or shortcomings. As a result, you push people away, even those who are close to you and important in your life.

With this trait, you do not allow much room for mistakes or failure. You standards are high, both for yourself and for others. You see the glass as half empty not half full. That is, you see what is wrong or problematic in situations where things are right as well.

Things have to be just right. While this trait could serve you well in certain professions or occupations—such as accountant, lettering artist, or sign painter—it works against you in human relationships. You alienate people with your need to control. You feel as though being in control of situations gives you a better chance at getting things done your way.

If you are too perfectionist, it is hard to relax. Enjoying your accomplishments is next to impossible because you see what you have not accomplished more clearly than what you have. In fact, you may even feel like an impostor because you have such high standards that you can never quite reach them, despite your competence and best efforts.

You can set yourself up to relapse or feel extremely bad if your perfectionism persists. Mistakes or setbacks in recovery will be blown out of proportion in your mind. Feelings of frustration and anxiety may build up as a result. Going back to your addictive behavior may seem like an attractive alternative if things build up too much.

But, like any other trait, perfectionism too can be changed. This is Bill's description of how he changed his perfectionism. "My dad was a perfectionist. He had high expectations and never was one to give out praise. I think that's where I learned it. If I made five As and one B on a report card, he focused on the B. If I made five good plays and one error in a baseball game, he focused on the error. I started very early trying so hard to please him and win his approval. It's too bad because I could never do it.

"This whole thing spilled over to all areas of my life. I was never satisfied with anything I did. Or anything anybody else did, for that matter. I drove my wife and kids crazy with my picky ways. They could never do things to meet my strict standards. I think this messed up my youngest kid. He seems so insecure and afraid to try new things. My perfectionism even showed when I played golf or went bowling. I just couldn't enjoy a good game without criticizing my mistakes. I got frustrated pretty easy, even when having a good game. If I bowled a 220, I thought I should have bowled a 250.

"Over time, I learned to allow room for mistakes. In myself and others. At first, it was easier to cut others a break than myself. I had to focus on progress, not perfection, and give myself credit for things I did well.

"Part of my recovery was talking to my father about some of these things that flavored our relationship. It helped me get over some of my resentments toward him. I had to accept that he probably wouldn't change his perfectionistic ways. But, I didn't have to keep trying to meet his standards and get his approval. It only made me feel bad.

"I guess the biggest challenge was at home with my wife and kids. I had to back off and stop criticizing and controlling them. It was like starting from square one—I actually had to learn to give them praise for things they were doing. I had to learn to praise effort, not just results. Even if my kids weren't doing real well at something, I worked hard at trying to make them feel good about the efforts they were putting forth. I had been so achievement- and results-oriented that this was hard for awhile. I also worked hard to appreciate my wife's efforts. She was such a loving, good, and competent woman. It wasn't until I was well into my recovery from addiction that I could let her know how much I appreciated her. And to share positive comments with her.

"The idea of acknowledging efforts, not just results, was a big step forward for me. I tried to apply this to myself as well, not just my kids and wife. I always did most things quite well, but because of my perfectionism, I had serious trouble being kind to myself. Part of this also was revamping some attitudes about failure or mistakes. Learning these were normal, OK, and even a desirable part of life was an important lesson for me."

ANTISOCIAL

Those with addictions that involve illegal behaviors most commonly show antisocial traits. Having an expensive drug habit, for example, often leads a person into deviant activities to help support the addiction. Some compulsive gamblers who are deeply in debt may resort to antisocial behaviors in order to get money to cover their bets. Certain types of compulsive sexual behavior also may involve antisocial actions. With some people, stopping their addictions leads to a total or significant reduction of antisocial behavior. For such people this trait is part and parcel of the addiction. However, this is not always the case. Some people continue to be antisocial long after stopping the addictive behavior.

Antisocial behavior generally refers to going against society and doing things that are wrong, bad, and often against the law. If you are antisocial, you probably use people and take advantage of them. You probably lie, cheat, and con others to get what you want. You probably have little if any guilt about what you do or how you affect others. You look out for number one, that is all that really matters. Extreme cases of antisocial behavior may involve violent, cruel, or even evil behaviors toward others.

Matt, who is recovering from compulsive sexual addiction, shared some details about his antisocial trait and how he changed it. "Ever since I can remember, I was a con and a cheat. Growing up, I was always in trouble with my teachers, parents, and the law. I did a lot of things I'd prefer to forget. My fuse was pretty short, so I was always arguing or fighting with people.

"I also ripped people off a lot. Even stole from my grandmother, if you can believe that! Didn't trust no one and floated from one woman to the next. Used them all for my selfish needs—money, sex, convenience. When my sexual behaviors got real out of control, I was doing things I could get a lot of time for if I got busted.

"I was one of those sweet-talking guys who really seemed sincere. So I got away with a lot. And brother, do I mean a lot! Yeah, but things caught up with me and I ended up in big trouble a couple of years ago. In fact, that's how I got into treatment the first time.

"One night I went to a meeting and heard this guy speak. His story sounded a lot like mine. I couldn't believe how this guy had changed. And how he seemed to like himself now and how his life was going. It seemed unreal and I thought maybe he was a fake or something. But I talked with him after the meeting. He became my sponsor and I've been in recovery ever since.

"I won't lie and tell you I'm a mister goody two shoes now. There are some things I still mess up. But the conning, cheating, and law breaking have all stopped. I have respect for others and for society now. Part of my recovery is taking the message to others. It's always a stark reminder of where I came from. I see so many people messing up like I used to.

"Probably the biggest step forward in my recovery was admitting all the cons (at least the ones I remembered) and sharing them with others. This opened the door for me to change some sick attitudes about right and wrong. At first, it was weird being straight and honest. It didn't seem genuine. But, the longer I practiced this new behavior of not lying or conning, the more used to it I became.

"It helped to cut loose most of my running people. I don't mess with these people any more. It'll just pull me down. I hang around recovering people. They help keep me grounded since it's easy for me to lose track of where I've come from."

Self-Awareness Task 7–1: *Understanding Your Personality Traits*

Review the traits discussed in the previous sections. Which ones do you identify with the most? Why? Choose two of these traits that you want to work on changing. For each of these two traits, answer the following questions:

1. Where do you think this trait came from? Who or what life circumstances influenced this trait in you?
2. What are your beliefs, attitudes, or thoughts about this trait? (That is, when you think about this trait, what exactly comes to mind?)
3. How does this trait show in your behaviors (at home, work, or school, or with friends, and so on)?
4. How has this trait helped you?
5. What problems has this trait caused in your life?
6. Why do you need to, or want to, change this trait?
7. What specifically can you do to change this trait?
8. What potential benefits might you gain if you change this trait?

Other Traits

Early in this chapter I mentioned that I would cover some of the more common traits, rather than all of them. An entire book could be written just to discuss these various traits.

Keep in mind that traits are descriptors that can be used to characterize you in general, not just in one particular situation. The idea of focusing on your traits is to build on your strengths and improve your weaknesses so that you decrease your possibility of relapsing.

The following list gives some additional traits. Check those with which you identify, both positive and negative. You can use the same questions posed in Self-Awareness Task 7–1 to help you begin to understand and change these traits.

Angry or hostile   Empathetic or nonempathetic

Anxious   Sensual or passionate

Depressed	Serious
Negative (or positive)	Playful
Indifferent	Aloof or detached
Dramatic	Shallow or superficial
Sensitive	Tough or rugged
Hypersensitive	Soft
Jealous	Persistent
Insecure	Ambitious
Loving or affectionate	Lazy
Kind or caring	Indecisive
Loyal and committed	

Regardless of the specific traits you wish to change, some general principles can help you with this process. Many of the stories of change in this chapter illustrate these principles with a variety of people. These specific principles are outlined in the following list.

- *Try to understand the sources of each trait: how and where you got it.* Many traits have their roots in early childhood and were developed in your family of origin. Try to think about how much you are like your mother, father, or other caretaker in regard to each trait you evaluate. Look at other contributing factors as well. Your family is not the only source of influence. However, more than cultural or psychological factors can influence your personality or character. Biological factors may contribute to some traits.

- *Change your attitudes and thoughts about these traits.* Often, before a change can be translated into behavior, you have to change how you think about what you are changing. Your values, attitudes, or thoughts may first have to change. On the other hand, sometimes changes in attitudes or values come only after you change the behavior associated with a given trait.

- *Make amends to other significant people who have been hurt by your particular personality trait.* This can help undo some of the damage or bad feelings created by your past behavior, reduce your feelings of guilt, and improve your relationships.

- *Translate your desire to improve your personality to actual changes in your behaviors.* No matter how small or seemingly insignificant, make some actual changes in your actions or behaviors. Sometimes you have to go slowly and start with minor changes. You can then build on these and make more significant changes later.

- *Evaluate your changes on an ongoing basis.* This can help you see your progress and set the stage for you to reward yourself for changing. It can also help you spot problems or rough spots, or help you see when you are returning to an old pattern of behavior.

- *Remember: as difficult as it seems to change a personality trait, it is possible.* But only through commitment and work. Use others to guide you if needed—sponsors in self-help programs, counselors, or other professionals who work with you in therapy.

- *Use a guide if needed.* Although you can make changes as part of a program of self-management, you can also benefit from the knowledge, wisdom, and experience of others, such as a sponsor in a self-help program, a professional therapist, or another person whom you trust.

- *Use the twelve-step program to help you change your character.* As discussed previously, the twelve-step program of the self-help organizations (listed at the end of this book) can be a potent change mechanism. Use this program to your advantage to build on your strengths and work on your weaknesses of character.

8

Key Issues in Family and Interpersonal Relationships

Y OUR relationships with family, friends, and other people play a very important role in your recovery as well as in your overall satisfaction in life. Satisfying your emotional needs depends to a large extent on the type and quality of relationships you have with other people. Without close and satisfying relationships you are likely to be unhappy and frustrated. You may even feel empty or lonely. On the other hand, if you have solid interpersonal relationships you will reap many benefits and your life will be more complete.

One of the many functions of mutual relationships is giving and getting support or help. Others may lean on you for love, nurturance, support, advice, or practical help. And you may do the same with them. As mentioned in chapter 2, your family and social relationships are very pertinent to your recovery from an addictive disease or behavior. Dealing with such interpersonal recovery issues helps to build the foundation for your ongoing recovery and, in turn, can reduce the chances of relapse in a number of ways. First, you can reduce the possibility of important people in your life sabotaging your recovery by enabling, pressuring, or even covertly influencing you to return to your addictive disorder. Second, dealing with these interpersonal recovery issues paves the way for you to develop a relapse-prevention network of family and friends on whom you can depend to support your recovery. Others are more likely to help you (and not sabotage your recovery) if you deal with them honestly on these interpersonal issues. And third, if your emotional needs are satisfied through healthy relationships you will feel less need to resort to your addictive behavior to meet your needs.

The importance of relationships is evident in the literature about recovery because much emphasis is placed on the importance of family and personal relationships in recovery. This importance is also evident in the twelve-step program of the self-help organizations. Two steps specifically address your impact on others. Step eight states, "Made a list of all persons we had harmed and became willing to make amends to them all." This step helps you acknowledge that others have indeed been harmed and identify these individuals by making a list of who they are. Step eight also focuses on your attitude and asks you to become willing to make amends. Such willingness is an act of courage and, although not easy to do, can help your recovery immensely. Not being willing to make amends is rather selfish and could possibly interfere with your long-term recovery and your interpersonal relationships.

Step nine takes this acknowledgment and asks you to put the process of making amends into action. It states, "Made direct amends to such people wherever possible except when to do so would injure them or others." This step requires you to do something, to take some type of action. However, you are advised not to attempt making amends if doing so would be counterproductive and hurt another person. For example, if you sexual or gambling addiction had inflicted tremendous emotional pain on your former spouse, trying to make amends could open up old wounds and bring back bad thoughts and feelings. If the relationship has ended, then you are better off letting things go. Focus instead on the relationships that are still a part of your life at the present time.

Because of the importance of interpersonal issues in recovery and relapse prevention, several of these issues will be discussed in this chapter.

Understanding the impact of your addiction on others

Making amends

Love, intimacy, and friendship

Mutuality in relationships

Resolving conflicts and differences in relationships

Appreciating differences

Communication and feedback

Fun, enjoyment, and spontaneity

The remainder of this chapter will focus on these key interpersonal issues in recovery. In chapter 9, the practical and emotional aspects of building your relapse-prevention network will be discussed.

Understanding Your Impact on Others

Since you cannot function in society without being involved in significant relationships with others, there is little doubt that your addiction has had an impact on other people in your life. These people include, but certainly are not limited to, your family, close friends, and people whom you have worked with or associated with for some common interest or goal. Usually, the people most affected are those who are closely involved with you emotionally or those with whom you come in contact most frequently.

The impact your addiction has had on other people may vary from slight or little impact to very profound. The actual impact will depend on a variety of factors, such as how long you have had your addiction, how bad it was, and how it affected your attitudes, feelings, and behaviors toward others. For example, if your addiction contributed to making you deceitful, manipulative, and violent toward your family or friends, your behavior would have a different impact than if you did not act in any of these ways. Or, if your addiction caused you to spend too much of the family income, or ignore the needs of your spouse or children, this behavior also will have a different impact on your family. In addition, your impact on others will be mediated by their perception of you—that is, how they view you. Two people could have been exposed to very similar behaviors on your part, yet each may view you in an entirely different manner.

Virtually any aspect of a person's life can be affected, either directly or indirectly, by your addiction and related behaviors.

These effects can be on their physical, mental, or spiritual health; their financial security; or their attitudes and behaviors. The emotional burden can be very heavy and they may suffer tremendously on the inside—even if they present themselves differently on the outside. The wife of a compulsive gambler, for example, can be devastated by her husband's gambling. She may feel angry, resentful, powerless, very worried, sad, and depressed. Yet, it is possible that she could present herself to others, including her husband, as doing just fine. The internal pain people undergo is not always communicated to others.

In terms of your family, you can have an impact on the family system as well as on its individual members. Your addiction and related behaviors could have affected the mood or tone of your family, how it feels to be part of it, how people act toward each other, the roles they assume, how they act while fulfilling these roles, how they communicate and interact, and the quality of their relationships. Your addiction could also have affected your family's reputation as well as its financial security.

Many families involved with an addicted person experience a sense of loss. They feel cheated out of time, interest, and support. The longer your addiction and the more it dominated your life, the more intensely your family probably has suffered. Your family members may have structured their lives around you, even during periods in which you did not engage in your addiction.

Your family members can get as "addicted" to you as you were to your addiction. Experts refer to this process as codependency. Because of codependency, family members often show their own problematic behavior. They may have lied or covered up for you, or done other things that enabled your addiction to continue. They may have felt a range of emotions on the inside and harbored much negative feeling toward you. Their integrity and self-esteem may have been harmed. Codependency may show in virtually any area of their lives.

Because of these and other adverse effects of family members on an addicted member, they often need to participate in recovery themselves. This provides them with the chance to grow, change, get over their emotional wounds, and develop healthier behaviors. Self-help programs for families have been created specifically to help them deal with their codependency recovery issues. Many family members benefit from professional treatment as well. Inpatient codependency programs and outpatient therapies are available.

The effects of addiction on a family are not all negative. Many positive consequences may also occur. For example, perhaps your family members banded closer together as they coped with your addiction. Or maybe they learned to depend on themselves and satisfy their needs through someone besides you. Usually, the effects of addiction on your family include a combination of negative and positive factors.

Self-Awareness Task 8–1: *Evaluating the Effects of Your Addiction on Your Family*

Describe how you think your addiction and related behavior affected your family unit. Give the negative as well as the positive effects.

Describe how individual members (parents, spouse, siblings, other relatives) of your family were affected by your addiction. Give the negative as well as the positive effects.

If you have children, describe how they were affected by your addiction. Give the negative as well as the positive effects.

Who in your family was most affected by your addiction?

Have you ever openly discussed your addiction and recovery with your family members? If yes, what were the results? If no, why not?

Self-Awareness Task 8–2: *Evaluating the Effects of Your Addiction on Your Friendships or Personal Relationships*

List other people whom you believe were most hurt by your addiction and related behaviors.

For each of these people, describe the specific ways in which they were affected by you.

Which of your relationships was most harmed by your addiction?

Have you lost important friendships or personal relationships as a result of your addiction and related behaviors? If so, how?

What impact has losing relationships because of your addiction had on you?

Making Amends

Once you acknowledge the people who have been hurt in one way or another by your addiction, you can then decide whether or not you need to do something to make amends for what you have done. Usually, amends are made to those people who are still a significant part of your life—those with whom you maintain a relationship.

Many people in recovery have found making amends to be a helpful and significant part of their recovery. Making amends can benefit the person to whom it is directed, as well as yourself. It may make you feel less guilty and shameful about your past behaviors. Forgiving yourself may become easier, too. And making amends can be a factor in decreasing the chances of future relapse. Reducing conflict and improving your relationships are bound to help you in one way or another.

There is no right way to make amends. Some people believe that stopping the addiction is enough and that simply being in recovery is the best way of making amends. Others feel that they must make amends by some action or behavior to make up for some of what they did. Making amends may take more than one action on your part and may require a series of actions occurring gradually over time. An action may involve a simple gesture on your part or it may be complex and involved. What kind of action you take depends on what you have done to hurt the other person, what you think needs to be done to begin repairing the damaged relationship, and how you think the other person will respond to your efforts. Amends may come in the form of a heart-to-heart discussion during which your addiction and its impact on the other person are talked about openly and frankly. It sometimes helps to discuss specific things you did (or failed to do) that hurt the other person. Amends may involve apologizing for your past behaviors, repaying money borrowed or stolen, or fulfilling obligations or responsibilities that had previously been ignored.

Sometimes it is impossible to make amends for all that you did during your addiction. For example, if your addiction caused you to spend very little time with your spouse or children, an apology could never suffice to make up for what they missed from you. In this situation, you can try to make amends by showing them that you want the present and future to be different. You can take an active interest in their lives, spend time with them, and work to meet their needs. You can encourage them to get involved in recovery programs for families if you think they need it. Such involvement can lessen the chances that others will hold grudges or throw the past up in your face. In such cases, amends are made by changing how you act in your relationships with others at the present time.

If you make amends to another person, you are advised to do so because you want to and because it is the right thing to do. Just be sure that you are sincere in your efforts to make amends. Making amends is something into which you should put a lot of thought and effort.

Making amends may bring you closer to others. Others may let go of their anger and forgive you more easily if they perceive that you genuinely are sorry for what you did to them. These examples are just a few of the many potential benefits of making amends.

On the other hand, there are risks in making amends as well. Others may not want to hear what you have to say; they may become upset and angry with you; or they may be so fed up and disgusted that nothing you do could change their thoughts and feelings. Although you can try to anticipate how they may react, you cannot be entirely sure of how they will react once you make a gesture of amends. Generally, however, people are willing to forgive and will be open to your efforts. Do not be surprised if they also appreciate your willingness to make amends.

Self-Awareness Task 8–3: *Making Amends*

Toward whom have you attempted to make amends?

How did you feel both before and after attempting to make amends?

Were any people unreceptive to your gestures to make amends? If yes, who were they and why do you think they would not accept your efforts at making amends?

For those who were receptive to your amends, what impact did this have on you?

What impact did this have on your relationship with them?

Self-Awareness Task 8–3: *Continued*

Are there significant people in your life with whom you have not yet made amends? If yes, why not? Do you plan to do so in the future?

If you have not yet made amends, what is your reason?

Do you believe that staying in recovery in and of itself is sufficient and that no other direct actions are needed on your part to make amends?

Key Issues in Your Interpersonal Relationships

One of the many benefits that recovery brings is the opportunity to improve your relationships with other people. This benefit can directly or indirectly enhance your recovery as well as reduce the chances of relapsing to your addiction. For instance, if you nurture your relationship with your partner and gain increasing emotional satisfaction, you may feel less need to escape into your addiction in an attempt to temporarily feel better or deal with upsetting emotions. If you learn to resolve differences, problems, and negative feelings, they will become less of a force in triggering a desire to return to your addictive behavior to escape, get even, or blot out emotional pain.

In the following sections I will discuss issues in your interpersonal relationships. Since it would be impossible to discuss all of these issues in depth, I will focus on key issues that appear fairly commonly among people with addictions.

LOVE, INTIMACY, AND FRIENDSHIP

You have a need to love and be loved; you also need friendship and intimacy—closeness to others. These are some of the most basic and essential of all of your human needs. An addiction can function as a substitute for intimacy and closeness in relationships. Recovery therefore involves learning to satisfy these needs through your relationships with others rather than through your addiction. Satisfying your needs for love, intimacy, and friendship should reduce your chances of relapse.

One immediate difficulty in talking about love is that it can mean many different things, depending on the relationship. When you say that you love your spouse, it normally means something different than when you say you love your parents, your child, or a friend.

Addiction interferes with your love relationships. Although making amends can help repair some of the damage of the past, it is essential to take actions to nurture your love relationships. It is not enough to feel love toward others; you need to show it through your behaviors or actions. Words of love are meaningless if not backed up by attitudes and behaviors.

You may use the term love generically, although in reality there are different types of love. They share some similarities, but have differences as well.

First is romantic love, in which you feel strong emotion toward another person. You feel tender and passionate, and want to be with the object of your romantic love. You share closeness and intimacy and know each other well. This is the type of love shared between partners in a committed relationship, for example, in a marriage or in a homosexual union.

Second is erotic love, which refers to love based on sensual or sexual feelings. This type of love usually has both physical and emotional components. Romantic love and erotic love usually are felt toward the same person.

Third is friendship love, which is based on sharing interests, goals, common concerns, and companionship with another. Mutually satisfying and respectful relationships with friends will enhance your enjoyment of recovery. The more you satisfy your needs in a mature manner through your friendships, the less need you will have to seek temporary satisfaction through your addiction. Making amends to friends who were hurt by your addiction and actively working at nurturing these friendships can improve the quality of your life. Involvement in twelve-step recovery programs provides you with a tremendous opportunity to develop this type of love with others in recovery. Everyone potentially benefits, particularly if the friendship is mutual rather than centered on the needs of only one individual in the relationship.

Fourth is dependent love, which develops when you fulfill the needs of another person, such as a child. Or dependent love can characterize an interdependent relationship with another, such as a spouse or lover, in which each fulfills the other's needs. Interdependency implies mutuality and balance, with each person depending on the other and being depended upon. Although there are boundaries between you, and each has personal space, there is also the ability to mutually share. Dependent love with an adult is problematic when it becomes excessive or too one-sided.

Last is altruistic love, which refers to unselfish concern for the well-being of another person. This type of love shows less in feeling and more in actions—giving to others and trying to make a difference. This type of love is frequently seen in recovery programs, where people help each other. In fact, it is seen in step twelve of the twelve-step recovery program, which says, "Having had a spiritual awakening as the result of these steps, we tried to carry this message to [alcoholics, drug addicts, sex addicts, compulsive gamblers, or compulsive eaters] and to practice these principles in all our affairs." Recovering addicts who help others say they are helping themselves when they do it; but there is no denying that reaching out to a fellow human who suffers with a similar addiction is truly an act of caring and love. As recovery progresses, you are in a better position to give something to others. You may find that this also helps your recovery and further reduces the chances of relapse.

Self-Awareness Task 8–4: *Evaluating Your Love Relationships*

Is there enough love in your life today? If not, why?

Describe your need to give love and to receive love.

Describe the role love plays in your life at the current time.

Which of the types of love discussed in this book are most prevalent in your life today?

Is there a reasonable degree of balance among the different types of love in your life? If not, why?

Is there a reasonable degree of balance in your life in terms of giving and getting love?

Which type of love is most important to you?

How would others describe your ability to show love in your actions or behaviors?

What do you wish to change about your love relationships? How can you go about making this change?

MUTUALITY IN RELATIONSHIPS (GIVE AND TAKE)

Give and take is another important aspect of interpersonal relationships. This process implies reciprocity or mutuality, not one-sidedness. You not only get or take from others to meet your needs, but you also give to them as well. If your relationships are one-sided, and you are only a taker or a giver, then they will be problematic and less satisfying.

Takers often push other people away with their self-centeredness and their incessant need to get. Givers, on the other hand, create far fewer problems with others. Their main problem is within themselves. They often secretly resent others and can become passive-aggressive as a way of dealing with negative feelings toward other people.

Everyone knows people who tend to be primarily givers or takers. You may think about someone specific in your life who fits into one of these categories. How do you feel about him or her? What is the behavior like? How does this behavior affect you?

If you view yourself as too much of a taker, you can do many things to work on changing. For one thing, you can pay attention to your conversations with others and consciously work at listening more to what others have to say, rather than talking too much. You can ask them questions about their lives and not always turn the conversation back to what you think or what is going on in your life. Altering other areas of your behavior can also help. You may do things for others, such as calling them on the phone to say hello or ask how they are doing, visiting them, sending cards or letters, or giving gifts. Remember, though, that giving of yourself will be received more positively than giving something like a gift.

Self-Awareness Task 8–5: *Evaluating Mutuality in Your Relationships*

How would you evaluate your general pattern of relationships in terms of give and take?

Is there a balance of give and take in most of your relationships? If not, why not?

Is mutuality more of a problem in some relationships than others? If yes, which ones and why?

Are you more of a giver than a taker? If yes, why?

If you are more of a giver than taker, what effect does this have on your relationships? On your satisfaction with yourself or your life?

Are you more of a taker than a giver? If yes, why?

If you are more of a taker than a giver, what effect does this have on your relationships? On your satisfaction with yourself or your life?

What steps can you take to achieve a better balance in your relationships in terms of give and take?

What are the potential benefits if you work at changing the balance in your relationships in terms of give and take?

RESOLVING CONFLICTS AND PROBLEMS

A critical issue in relationships is resolving conflicts and problems in a way that is acceptable and reasonable to all the people involved. Conflict resolution helps prevent negative feelings from building up. As you may remember from earlier discussions, negative feelings, such as anger and resentment, are very common factors contributing to relapse in addictive disorders. So dealing with problems directly is a good way of ensuring that feelings do not get stuffed and later result in a relapse.

Resolving conflicts helps you feel better about yourself and the people with whom you are involved in mutual relationships. Other people may also feel better about their relationships with you when conflicts are faced head on and resolved. When you feel good about yourself and your relationships, it is easier to seek support or help from others when you need it. And this positive attitude puts you in a better position to satisfy some of your other needs, such as for love, closeness, or intimacy. Obviously, it is difficult for anyone to give to someone with whom they are upset, angry, or have unresolved problems or conflicts.

Dealing with conflicts and problems in relationships requires an open attitude and a willingness to risk saying what is on your mind. Many addicts talk about not wanting to "upset the apple cart," so to speak, so they stuff their feelings and avoid conflict at all costs. This tendency only causes more problems in the long run. Sometimes attitudes about conflicts and problems in relationships must change before your behavior can change.

In everyday life you can find many reasons to avoid dealing directly with conflict. Although certainly there are instances in which avoidance of direct conflict is the best approach, in most instances this is probably not the case. Conflicts with the people you live with or relate to closely and regularly should be acknowledged and faced. Otherwise, expect resentments to build.

Understanding and appreciating the other person's point of view helps in resolving conflicts. If you are completely certain that you are right and the other person is wrong about a specific problem, you are less likely to resolve things. Sometimes the resolution of problems is simply to accept that each of you has different viewpoints about the issue at hand. You both can be right in your positions. When you see the other person's viewpoints, you put yourself in a better position to make compromises, even when the final result is that you and another person agree only that you disagree.

Conflict resolution does not mean always giving in to the other person. If you always are giving in or compromising, rest assured that this will bother you deep inside. Sometimes, in certain conflicts, you should hold your ground and not give in or compromise.

Other important aspects of conflict resolution include listening closely to others and respecting what they say, expressing your thoughts and feelings about the situation at hand, taking responsibility only for yourself and not other people, and confronting differences in an open and mature manner. Do not expect the process always to go smoothly. Be prepared to deal with some situations in which there are no clear-cut resolutions of conflict. However, by taking some of the afore-mentioned steps, you can increase the chances of resolving conflicts and problems in relationships with other people.

Self-Awareness Task 8–6: *Evaluating Your Style of Conflict Resolution*

Describe your usual style of dealing with conflicts or problems with other people. Also describe how your style affects your life.

Is your style generally to avoid conflict? If yes, why? (That is, what are you most concerned about if you get into conflicts with others?)

If you usually avoid conflict, what effect does this have on your physical and mental health and on your level of satisfaction with your interpersonal relationships?

Is your style generally to be very confrontational when experiencing conflicts with others? If yes, why?

If you are confrontational, what effect does this have on your health and level of satisfaction with your interpersonal relationships?

What do you need or want to change about how you handle conflict? What specific steps will you take to implement these changes?

COMMUNICATION AND FEEDBACK

Effective communication involves many different elements. One key element is self-disclosure, which is how you talk about yourself to others. Self-disclosure also occurs through your actions (for example, how you dress, your leisure activities, who you socialize with, and so on) and in your body language and tone of voice. This process lets others know about you on a variety of levels.

Poorly adjusted people tend to share too much or too little of themselves in relationships. They may, for example, share very private aspects of their lives with people they hardly know. Well-adjusted people are flexible and share a lot of personal things with selected people and moderate amounts of personal things to others. They are discreet, and know when and where it is right to share details of their private thoughts, feelings, or experiences.

Because good communication is two-sided, listening to what others say is another important skill. This skill allows you to see things from other people's perspectives and to put yourself in their shoes. Such understanding helps you be empathetic or sensitive to their needs and experiences. Although the notion of listening seems very basic, many people do not know how to truly listen to others. Listening involves hearing not only the content of what others say, but also the feelings behind the words. This kind of listening requires an awareness of the other person's nonverbal behavior.

Listening closely to others makes it easier to respond to what they are saying in a way that shows you understand them. Responding is most effective when it does not evaluate or judge others. Good responses simply validate what people are saying and convey a sense of understanding them, regardless of whether or not you agree with them. You can respond with body cues as well as with words when responding to others. In fact, your body cues may give a completely different message from your words.

Confronting conflicts and differences is probably the most difficult interpersonal skill of all. As I mentioned previously, many people like to avoid differences and hence do not confront others. Although you may think of confrontation as an attack on others, it really means an invitation to have a dialogue and openly discuss feelings, thoughts, behaviors, or experiences and their consequences. Confrontation allows you to get and receive feedback from others. Feedback is a way of checking how others see you or letting them know how you see them. Ideally, the feedback process will give you information about yourself that you can use to make changes in your interpersonal style.

Self-Awareness Task 8–7: *Evaluating Your Style of Communication*

Describe your style of self-disclosure to others.

Do you share too much with too many people? If so, why? How does this affect your relationships?

Do you share too little of yourself with others? If so, why? How does this affect your relationships?

Self-Awareness Task 8–7: *Continued*

Describe your style of listening to others.

How would others describe your style of listening to them? Would they see you as a good listener? Poor? Or a combination?

Describe your style of challenging or confront-ing others.

What role does feedback play in your inter-personal relationships?

What is one change you want or need to make in your communication style? How will you go about making this change? What are the potential risks and benefits?

As I mentioned at the beginning of this chapter, many dif-ferent issues are important in interpersonal relationships, both in terms of supporting your recovery as well as adding to your satisfaction in life. This chapter specifically focused on some of the more common issues relevant to recovery and relapse pre-vention. There are many other important interpersonal issues, however, and you need to keep this in mind as you work at your ongoing recovery. Some of these include learning to appreciate differences with others, building fun and enjoyment in relation-ships, and being spontaneous—to name just a few.

Learning to appreciate and enjoy differences between your-self and others can enrich your life. Such differences may be in philosophy, opinions, lifestyle, cultural background, interests, or interpersonal style. It would be boring if everyone thought, acted, or lived the way we do.

Fun and enjoyment are key variables in interpersonal satis-faction as well. The ways in which fun and enjoyment can be built into your life are endless. You can enjoy many activities, interests, hobbies, and avocations. And the more you experience natural fun and enjoyment, the less vulnerable you may be to relapse to your addiction.

The last issue I wish to mention is spontaneity, the ability to do things on the spur of the moment, without prior planning. The ability to be spontaneous and create special moments to enjoy with others can add joy to your life. Sometimes, the particular activity that you engage in spontaneously is less important than the process of engaging in it. Being spontaneous makes you feel free, vibrant, and alive.

9

Building Your Relapse-Prevention Network

A RELAPSE-PREVENTION network (RPN) includes the people on whom you can lean for help and support. These are people who know that you are recovering from an addiction and who are willing to help you. These are people with whom you can take the initiative and reach out for help or support. They are also people who know you well enough and care about you enough to tell you directly if they think you are in a relapse process or failing in your recovery.

The sections that follow present some suggested steps you can follow in building your RPN. Keep in mind that while other people can support or help you, your recovery is not their responsibility. Ultimately, only you can take responsibility for your recovery.

Gaining Help and Support from Others
WHO TO INVOLVE

Your RPN can include family members, friends, coworkers, your sponsor in a self-help program, or other recovering individuals with whom you come into regular contact. These should be people with whom you have some type of mutual relationship. Try to avoid one-sided relationships in which you only seek help and support from others without giving something back. An RPN should include people you trust and can talk with openly and honestly about recovery issues or a potential relapse. They should be people whom you think do not hold resentments against you. Your RPN may include a few people or many. People who understand addiction and recovery will probably be the most helpful. Some types of addictions, such as compulsive sexual behavior, require you to be especially discreet about whom you ask for help.

ASKING FOR SUPPORT

A proactive approach to relapse prevention is one in which you take the initiative and engage others in discussions relevant to your recovery. There is no single way and no easy way to do this. Many people find this step much easier to think about and plan than to actually implement. Asking for help or support is not easy.

One way to ask for support is to be forthright. State directly that you are working hard at recovery and wish to enlist the person's support as part of your relapse-prevention network. Give such people information about the concept of relapse prevention and answer any questions that they raise.

Many people find it helpful to practice asking for support before carrying it out in real life. This technique has several advantages. First, it gives you some experience in choosing words you can use to engage another in a discussion of relapse prevention. This kind of rehearsal can raise your comfort and confidence level. Second, this technique allows you to work out some of the difficulties that go along with trying something new. If you get hung up over exactly what to say, you can work on the rough edges through practice. This practice allows you to find words and a style that fit you. Third, practice raises your awareness of the emotional issues involved in requesting help from others. Perhaps you feel weak, anxious, embarrassed, or shameful. Knowing this ahead of time gives you a chance to work through these feelings so that when the situation really arises you do not abandon your plan because of your emotional reactions. And finally, practice gives you a chance to anticipate how others may respond. You can then better prepare for how to handle possible reactions from others.

When you practice asking for support, it sometimes helps to play the role of the person whom you will ask. You can use your knowledge of them to anticipate their probable reactions. Playing the roles of other people can have the added benefit of giving you a better sense of what they may think and feel.

Since other people are under no obligation to help or support your recovery efforts, you should also think about how to deal with those who refuse to help you. Try to respect their decision, understand why they will not help or support you, and do not make them feel guilty. When you take a risk and reach out for help, you must remember that others have a right to refuse. Let them know that this is an option if you think it would help them save face.

TELLING OTHERS HOW YOU THINK THEY CAN HELP

Think about exactly what others can do to help or support you. What do you want from them? Is your request realistic and fair? If you keep in mind that recovery is your responsibility, you may offer your suggestions on how the other person can help you.

You can request help specifically related to a desire or impulse to engage in your addiction. Or you may ask for help in less direct ways. For example, you could ask a family member or friend to do enjoyable things with you that do not put you at risk of relapse and that serve as healthy substitutes for your addiction.

The following examples illustrate telling others your ideas on how they can help.

- "Dave, I feel more vulnerable to binging when we keep a lot of sweets and junk food in the house. Can we talk about this so that you and the kids still have treats but I don't have to feel so threatened? I'd like you guys to keep the sweets in another cupboard so that I don't constantly see them when I open up the main food cupboard. Also, it would help if you would eat your snacks in the kitchen rather than bring them to the bedroom at night. When you bring ice cream and other desserts upstairs and eat in front of me, I sometimes struggle."
- "Kathy, my pattern after being sober for a while is to start thinking that I can eventually drink again. This is when I

start buying beer and liquor and make up some excuse, such as 'it's for guests.' I also slack off on going to meetings and get critical of AA. When I'm slipping back to old habits I know I get critical with you and our kids. If you have any concerns about me falling back to bad habits and think I could be headed for a relapse, would you tell me straight out? And if I brush you off—which I've done many times before—and don't seem to want to listen, or if I deny what you are saying, please write me a note. Just say what your concerns are and put the note in my wallet. It might help me be more objective if I can think about what you see when I'm not around you."

- "Mom, I really want to stay off drugs. I think it'd help me a lot if you and dad learned more about what it's like to stop drugs. Would you come to a few NA meetings with me so you can see what the program involves? You know how stubborn dad is when I ask him things, so would you mind trying to get him to come to a few meetings as well? They have meetings for family members of drug addicts as well, and I think these could be helpful, too. I'd also like you to read this information booklet about recovery. We can talk about it after you've had a chance to read it."

- "Ann, sometimes I get these very powerful sexual impulses and want to act on them. It's like they become the central focus of my thoughts and I obsess about men. You know how much I love my husband and how I don't want to do anything to hurt him or myself. I've tried ignoring these strong sexual impulses, but sometimes it's so hard. I'd like to be able to call you to talk when I have these feelings. Sometimes, just talking is a good release and the impulse gets weaker. Plus, I know you've had these impulses before and understand what it's like. You've done well in your recovery and probably could teach me some of what you did to live with your desires without acting on them."

- "Don, you know I can't gamble no more. Messed me up real bad. Lost about everything I ever had. So I can't go to the races with you 'cause I'm afraid I'll want some action and will bet. Man, I can't even buy no lottery tickets. Gotta give it all up. Hey, what say we do some other things where I don't have to worry about gambling? Like goin' fishing. Or, to a ball game. We can have a good time and I won't have to bet."

You can also ask people whom you want to be part of your RPN to give you other ideas on how they think they can help you. They may come up with some very helpful and creative ideas that never crossed your mind. Just be sure that you continually guard against letting others take control of or responsibility for your recovery.

Developing an Action Plan

Throughout this book, much emphasis has been placed on *action*. Some people find it very helpful to put their action plan in writing. You can discuss the idea of a written plan with certain members of your RPN. For example, Larry, a recovering alcoholic, his wife, and his three sons wrote the following plan.

- If any family member observes a potential relapse warning sign with Larry, it will be shared with other family members. They will make a joint decision on whether or not what they observe should be shared with Larry. If they agree that he should be told what was observed, Kevin (the oldest son) will be the spokesperson and tell his dad what was actually seen by other family members.
- If Kevin feels his dad is brushing him off and not taking the feedback seriously, the family will meet as a group with Larry to give the feedback. Larry agrees to listen and hear everyone out before responding.
- Larry will tell his family what he will do about this warning sign. Family members are free to add their ideas.
- If warning signs appear to increase in number and frequency, Larry agrees to initiate a discussion with his AA sponsor and AA home group.

Action plans need not be written in stone; they can be changed or modified as needed. As circumstances change, so do plans. If an agreed action plan does not work, then you should work at developing new strategies.

Discussing Potential and Actual Lapses or Relapses

It goes without saying that discussing a potential lapse (the first episode of returning to the addictive behavior) or a potential relapse with your RPN will be much easier than discussing an actual one. The situation has not occurred, so the emotional reactions are not as strong. Talking about the possibility of a lapse or relapse helps keep the reality in front of you and others. Relapse certainly can happen to you, so the better prepared you are, the more likely you are to cut it off quickly if it actually happens.

Discussing an actual lapse or relapse can seem like a very threatening proposition. This is especially true if you feel like you have let down your family or another important person. If you lapsed or relapsed without their knowledge of it, this decision becomes even harder to make. After all, what would your spouse think if he or she knew you had relapsed into compulsive sexual behavior or gambling, particularly if your addiction had caused a lot of pain and hardship before? Similarly, what do you do with feelings such as shame, guilt, or self-disgust and thoughts such as "I'm a failure" or "I really let her [him] down" that often accompany a relapse? Or what do you do if your family previously had agreed to ask you to leave the house if you relapsed? Or what do you do if you are on probation or parole and a relapse is a clear violation of this?

Talking and sharing your experience can help reduce the internal pain, help you learn something from the experience, and help you strengthen your recovery program. If you are in therapy or a self-help program, a good place to begin is talking about a relapse with your therapist, sponsor, or other group members. You can then explore options in terms of who else, if anyone, you should discuss your relapse with.

What specifically should you talk about if you relapsed? In chapter 3 the relapse process was discussed and a number of relevant questions were posed (see pages 48–49). These questions can guide you in your discussions with others.

Self-Awareness Task 9–1: *Building Your Relapse-Prevention Network*

Which family members are supportive of you and would be willing to be part of your RPN?

Which other people in your life are supportive of your recovery (friends, sponsor, or fellow member of your self-help group) and would be willing to be part of your RPN?

Are there people with whom you are very close but whom you believe should be excluded from your RPN? If so, whom? Why should you exclude them?

For each significant person you will ask for support, how and when will you approach them? What will you say to them?

How exactly would you like others to help or support you in your recovery efforts?

Are you prepared to discuss specific ideas on how others can be of help to you?

How do you think you will react (your thoughts, feelings, and behaviors) if someone you seek support from is not interested in being part of your RPN?

Whom will you share your written relapse-prevention plan with?

Which people from your RPN should you discuss an actual lapse or relapse with? Why?

What are the potential advantages you can see of developing an RPN?

10

Learning from Mistakes: Dealing with Lapses and Relapses

CHANGE is not easy to make. Probably not a person on earth has not struggled and returned to a habit or behavior that he or she tried to change. Mistakes are a common part of life. In recovery, mistakes happen as well, even among highly motivated people. No one is immune from the possibility of a lapse or a relapse. The harsh reality is that you can return to your addictive behavior at any time. Studies show that the first several months are the time during which most relapses occur. Therefore, in the early months of recovery you should pay particular attention to possible relapse triggers.

A return can be a single episode of your addictive behavior, referred to as a lapse. Or you can return to your addiction and reach the point where it takes over your life again. This is referred to as a full-blown relapse.

Experiencing a Lapse or Relapse

LAPSES

Not all single slips, or lapses, end in a full-blown relapse. Some people find that a lapse shakes them up and gives them a dose of reality. It strengthens their resolve for recovery because they realize that they are vulnerable to return to their addictive behavior. The following examples show lapses among various addicted individuals.

- *Gambling.* "I hadn't gambled in over a year and a half. Then, at a major league baseball game, I bought three half-innings of a baseball pool for a buck apiece. I won fifteen bucks because the most runs were scored in one of the innings I picked. Thinking about winning, then actually winning gave me a little rush, even though it was only a few bucks. Then, I said to myself, 'What the hell are you doing? You shouldn't be betting, not even on a baseball pool.' Later that night, I talked this over with my wife and a friend who is also recovering from compulsive gambling. Had to remind myself that it's the first bet that leads to the second. And the third. And so on." —Ken, age 37.

- *Overeating.* "My husband and I spent the Christmas holidays with his parents. His mother is a fantastic cook and bakes delicious pastries. For the most part, I kept to my eating plan during our stay. But, on Christmas eve and Christmas day, I blew it and pigged out. My mother-in-law had such a fantastic spread, I just couldn't resist it. I ate much more than I should have, especially rich desserts. I gained less than two pounds from this minibinge and quickly gained control of my impulse to overeat. Seems like every couple of months or so, I have one of these little binges. Fortunately, I always seem to get control of myself before things get out of hand." —Laura, age 28.

- *Alcohol.* "For the first couple of years in my recovery, I had a rather unusual pattern. I would not drink at all for three or four months, then I'd tie one on and get drunk. But, I'd only get drunk once. About three years ago, I finally stopped this pattern." —Don, age 59.

- *Cocaine.* "After being off coke for about nine months, I ran into an old girlfriend unexpectedly. She invited me over to her house and offered me cocaine. After snorting just one line I thought, 'You're crazy, man. You better get the hell out of here.' So I got up and left. I didn't tell her why I was leaving. I never saw her again. When I was snorting the line of coke I thought about how my cocaine addiction had cost me my business and led to spending over two years in jail. It just wasn't worth it no more to do drugs." —Richard, age 35.

- *Sex.* "I'd had a fantastic recovery for over five years. My sexual compulsion was under control and I was reaping the many rewards of recovery. On a vacation trip out of town, I met a man who was extremely interesting and humorous, not to mention attractive and very sexy. I let him charm and seduce me, acting on an impulse. In retrospect, I never expected anything like this to happen because I worked so hard at putting my life back together. Until this slip, I had controlled all of my compulsive sexual urges and impulses. Fortunately, I didn't let this one incident lead to anything else. I stopped myself real quick by admitting my mistake, sharing my experience with my support network, and reminding myself of how far I had come. It was quite an eye-opening experience for me because I never in a million years thought I'd have impulsive sex." —Arlene, age 42.

As these brief cases show, a lapse can occur early in recovery or after years of recovery. It can be a single, isolated event, as in Arlene's case, or a lapse can be part of a long-term recurring pattern of periods of recovery followed by lapses, as in Don's case.

A lapse may involve losing control during the episode of engaging in the addictive behavior. The person may "pig out," like Laura did, or get drunk, like Don did. Or a lapse may involve engaging in the behavior without losing control during the episode. Richard, for example, did not lose complete control and get high on drugs. After snorting just one line of cocaine he got hold of himself and left the situation.

In these cases, each person stopped their lapse quickly. They used self-talk procedures, reminded themselves of their past, left the situation, or talked over their experiences with another person. If you should lapse, review all of the details of your experience. It often helps to share this with someone you trust who understands your addiction and who is not easily conned. Evaluating your lapses and learning from your mistakes should help you in the future.

How you think about and respond to a lapse determines whether or not it will continue and end up in a full-blown relapse. If you have thoughts such as, "I blew my recovery; I'm a failure. What's the use of trying?" you are likely to give up and continue your addictive behavior. If you believe, "I've lost it, and I can't gain control," you are also likely to continue. If you respond too emotionally to a lapse, you can set yourself to continue the addictive behavior. For example, strong feelings of guilt, shame, or despair can make you think there is no sense in stopping. Or you may think that your addictive behavior is a way to temporarily blot out your painful feelings.

AN EXCEPTION TO THE LAPSE RULE

There is an important exception to the lapse rule for some people with sexual addictions. If a sexual addiction includes behavior such as child molesting, a single episode of molesting would be much more serious than a single episode of drinking alcohol, waging a bet, or overeating. In this instance, a lapse would be defined as conscious desires for or fantasies of engaging in sexual activity with children.

RELAPSES

Relapse occurs when you go beyond a lapse and continue engaging in your addictive behavior. A full-blown relapse refers to returning to the level of involvement in your addiction that preceded your recovery. Some people who relapse get even more heavily involved in their addictions than they had been prior to recovery. The paths relapses may take can vary significantly.

As you may recall from chapter 3, before you actually engage in an addictive behavior following a period of recovery, relapse warning signs will show up. Knowing your warning signs and relapse risk factors puts you in a position to plan ahead so that you are prepared to interrupt the process before a lapse or relapse to your addictive behavior occurs. But, in case a lapse or relapse happens, you should be prepared to stop it.

Some people never relapse. Others relapse just once or twice. A significant number of people relapse several times and, within this group, many exhibit a long-term pattern of periods of re-covery and periods of relapses. They relapse many, many times.

The truth is that some of these people probably did not relapse in the true sense of the word. More than likely they continued their addiction and only put it on hold from time to time. A relapse can occur only if you were truly in recovery—if you had accepted your addiction and actually had been working on a program of abstinence from your compulsive behavior and on personal and lifestyle changes.

RELAPSES FROM THE INSIDE OUT

The following stories of relapse experiences depict what relapse is like from an addicted person's point of view. After a brief overview of the addictions and their effects on the individuals' lives, the relapse process will be described. Other lifestyle and personal factors impinging on their relapses also will be discussed to illustrate that relapses are indeed complex and multifaceted. Relapses often involve personal internal factors, lifestyle factors, and environmental or external factors.

Patricia, a drug addict, age 29. "I've been a drug addict since I was a teenager. Although I've used everything, my drugs of choice were heroin and cocaine mixed together. My addiction was responsible for my losing several jobs and my nursing license. I lost a lot of money, my car and driver's license, and my self-esteem. People shied away from me and I lost many relationships. I broke my parents' hearts and caused them years of grief and anxiety. I also had many seizures caused by drugs and once overdosed on heroin and almost died. I'd do anything to get dope. I traded clean needles that I stole from the hospital and I traded sex for drugs. Did a lot of things to demean myself so I could get drugs. Getting high was so important that I'd stoop to any level to get my shit.

"I've been in and out of treatment for about eight years. I finished two rehabilitation programs and spent three months in a halfway house. I've been detoxified six times in hospitals. I've been in women's treatment programs, outpatient counseling, and under psychiatric care. I've been in and out of both AA and NA.

My periods of recovery have improved over the years and I've gone from just a few months' clean time to about two years.

"My last relapse lasted about two months. It started when an old junkie friend came over. Even though we got into a big argument, I let him stay all night and had sex with him. I was very upset that this happened, but I blamed him instead of myself.

"About a week before this incident occurred, I had gone to the hospital for pain and excessive menstrual bleeding. I was given a 'scrip for percodens, but I didn't tell anyone, including my NA sponsor. I hadn't cashed it in and carried the 'scrip in my purse. After feeling upset and disgusted with myself for having sex with a man I really didn't like very much, I conjured up a lot of physical and emotional pain. Later that day I started an argument with my mother, knowing that this would add fuel to my relapse fire that was beginning to burn strong.

"As you can imagine, I felt lousy emotionally. So I said, 'I should get the prescription for the pills filled.' On the way to the drug store I felt tormented and said to myself, 'God help me.' and 'What should I do?' But, by the time I reached the drugstore I was telling myself that I 'deserved' the pills. So I got the 'scrip filled.

"I told myself the pills would relax and calm me down. Also, I kept telling myself I couldn't have sex unless I was high. I couldn't wait, so I popped two pills as soon as I got outside of the drug store. Believe it or not, I had 'control fantasies.' I told myself that 'I'll show these fucking people' [counselors and Narcotics Anonymous friends]. I did in fact control my pill use . . . for a few weeks. Then, I started drinking and snorting cocaine. Before you knew it I was shooting dope again. I quickly became a physical and mental wreck.

"Since I got hooked again and got sick as a dog going through withdrawal on my own, I went to the hospital to get detoxed. After I cleaned up and got stable, me and my counselor looked at my relapse and lifestyle very closely.

"We found a lot of things had contributed to my relapse. For one thing, I had been having a real rough time with my recovery. Seemed like all I ever did was work and go to NA meetings. I felt bored by all of this, like I wasn't having any fun at all. Also, I was working on a "step four" personal inventory and beat myself up pretty damn bad.

"Even though I was feeling all bored with my life and in a deep rut, I didn't say nothing to my counselor or NA sponsor. I felt guilty for lying to my sponsor and telling her everything was going OK. But I continued to do this over and over. My sponsor knew something was up because I was avoiding her and not returning her phone calls. I created lies and excuses and vehemently denied anything was wrong.

"Drugs and booze weren't my only problem. Sex was too. I kept picking up men in NA who were newcomers. Most of the guys I hooked up with weren't very serious about their recovery. That's probably why I chose them, 'cause I knew I could get over on them. You see, I was very manipulative and used my sweetness and innocence to con them. I surrounded myself with these guys and used them for sex and other things.

"My sponsor knew a little about my pattern of using men and advised me to stop, but I kept doing it. Not only did I use men, but I was great at playing the victim role. I could blame them for my bad feelings and problems. This way I could avoid responsibility for my actions.

"Deep down, I was a very angry person, seething on the inside. Using men was one way of exhibiting my anger, because I often did things to humiliate them."

Eugene, a compulsive gambler, age 55. "I gambled and carried on for over thirty years. Horse races, poker, casinos, numbers, ball games, lotteries . . . you name it, I did it! I can't tell you how much money I lost because of my gambling addiction. Probably hundreds of thousands of dollars. But, I can tell you I lost everything else I had. I was obsessed with gambling and was always chasing the elusive 'big win.' My family left me years ago. It took me many years to make amends to my kids and get them interested in being part of my life.

"I had over five years without gambling before I relapsed. I had been very active in GA, but replaced GA meetings with church even though GA friends told me to also stick with the program.

"Over a period of about five weeks a lot of changes happened with me. My attitudes about recovery and life became real negative. I felt down and quit caring about important things in my life. I built up resentments toward a bunch of people, sometimes for stupid little things. You could say I copped a bad attitude. Then, I acted nasty to others.

"Since I felt stressed out, I started smoking more cigarettes. I lied to friends and isolated myself. For over three weeks, I seriously thought about catching some action, maybe calling a bookie or going to the track. I was bored as hell and not having any fun. Three times I drove past the race track but didn't go in. The next time I drove to the track, I watched the races. But I didn't bet. Next time I went to the track I bet on a few races. Within two weeks I blew my entire savings of $7,500 and sold a few bonds and CDs I had been saving up.

"I told myself I had to do something to stop. I felt very bad and depressed. Lost my self-respect. Told myself, 'You're no good, ain't nothing but a failure.' I plea-bargained with God and asked, 'Why am I doing this?' I talked to my minister who told me to stop gambling and get back in GA.

"I'm back on the right track again and haven't bet in over a year. It was a rude awakening for me. In a strange way, my relapse helped me. My life had been shallow and I was very lonely inside because I didn't have any close relationships. Since my relapse, I've worked on changing that. I'm learning to open up and share my feelings with others. I don't isolate myself now."

As these cases show, many factors directly and indirectly contribute to a relapse. The experience of relapse has many internal and external components. It causes many thoughts and strong feelings, particularly after an extended period of good recovery.

Both Patricia and Eugene salvaged their recovery and picked up the pieces after their relapse. They reached out for help and made it a point to learn from their mistakes. Both used their relapse to help them look at things they needed to change in themselves and their lives.

THE EFFECTS OF LAPSES AND RELAPSES

The effects of a lapse or relapse can vary considerably. On one extreme are negative effects such as serious medical or psychiatric problems. Some relapses lead to loss of job, family, or other significant relationships. Sadly, some end in death or incarceration. For example, Bill is serving time because he cashed bad checks following his gambling relapse. Michael is also serving time in jail for stealing a physician's prescription pad and forging prescriptions for narcotic and tranquilizing drugs.

Families can be affected by relapses as well, especially if the relapse goes on for a long time. They may feel upset, angry, and even bitter. The physical, emotional, or financial toll on them can be great. If they have been through a relapse with you before, old feelings and memories may be triggered. They may question your ability or motivation to recover. They may be simply tired of the same pattern, over and over.

The effects of a lapse or relapse are not always extremely negative. Minor problems may result. In some cases, the relapse experience serves to motivate people to work harder in their recovery. But the potential is always there for serious damage, because no one can predict how long a relapse will go on or what kinds of problems and complications it will cause.

After getting back on the right track after a relapse, it should be evaluated in great detail and discussed with someone who understands addiction, recovery, and relapse, such as a counselor or sponsor. This helps you learn from relapses and prepare to avoid them in the future. It is also helpful for your family to talk about the relapse in terms of what relapse signs they saw and how they felt about the relapse. They need a chance to express their thoughts and feelings about what happened. If they do not get this chance, they may harbor resentment toward you.

Techniques for Coping
EMERGENCY RECOVERY CARD

Many people in recovery find it helpful to carry an index card or paper in their purse or wallet with a list of names and phone numbers of people who can be called on in times of difficulty. This card may also list specific steps to take if a lapse or relapse occurs.

The following list gives the recommendations of several experts on what to do if a lapse or relapse occurs.

Stop, look, and listen.

Keep calm.

Renew your commitment to recovery.

Review the situation leading to the lapse or relapse.

Make an immediate plan for recovery.

Ask for help.

DAILY RELAPSE: PREVENTION INVENTORY

Another helpful technique is taking a daily inventory in which you use the following questions to guide the development of a plan of action.

At the start of the day: Do you anticipate any high-risk situations today that represent a threat to your recovery? If yes, what is your plan to deal with these situations?

At the end of the day: Were there any clues or warning signs present today suggesting that you are heading toward a lapse or relapse? If yes, what is your plan of action to stop a relapse from happening?

Self-Awareness Task 10–1: *Lapse and Relapse Interruption*

If you lapsed or relapsed before, describe what happened and what it was like for you (your thoughts, feelings, and subsequent behaviors; the effect on your self-esteem).

What was it like for your family, and how did they react?

If you never experienced a lapse or relapse, describe what it would be like (what you would think and feel, how it would affect your subsequent behaviors, and the effects on your self-esteem).

What would it be like for your family?

What is your plan of action to stop a lapse?

What is your plan of action to stop a relapse?

Who have you shared this plan with? If no one, why not?

Bibliography

Following is a list of books, articles, or guides that were consulted in the preparation of this book, as well as additional recommended readings. Separate listings are provided for professional therapists or care-givers and for individuals recovering from an addictive disorder.

BOOKS FOR PROFESSIONALS

Agras, M. W. 1985. *Panic: Facing fears, phobias and anxiety.* New York: W. H. Freeman.

American Psychiatric Association. 1987. *Diagnostic and statistical manual of mental disorders.* 3d ed. Washington, D. C.: American Psychiatric Association.

Annis, H., J. Graham, and C. Davis. 1987. *Inventory of drinking situations user's guide.* Toronto: Addiction Research Foundation of Ontario.

Beck, A. 1976. Cognitive therapy and the emotional disorders. NY: New American Library.

———. 1985. *Anxieties and phobias.* New York: Basic Books.

Beck, A. T., and G. D. Emery. 1977. *Cognitive therapy of substance abuse.* Philadelphia, Penn.: Center for Cognitive Therapy.

———. (1985). *Anxiety disorders and phobias: A cognitive perspective.* New York: Basic Books.

Beck, A., A. Rush, B. Shaw, and G. Emery. 1979. *Cognitive therapy of depression.* New York: Guilford Press.

Brown, S. 1985. *Treating the alcoholic: A developmental model of recovery.* New York: John Wiley and Sons.

Burns, D. 1980. *Feeling good: The new mood therapy.* New York: New American Library.

———. 1990. *The feeling good handbook.* New York: Penguin Books.

Carnes, P. 1984. *The sexual addiction.* Minneapolis, Minn.: CompCare.

Cohen, S. 1988. *The chemical brain: The neurochemistry of addictive disorders.* Irvine, Calif.: Care Institute.

Coleman, E., ed. 1987. *Chemical dependency and intimacy dysfunction.* New York: Haworth.

Cummings, C., J. R. Gordon, and G. A. Marlatt. 1980. *Relapse: Prevention and prediction.* In W. R. Miller, ed. The addictive behaviors. New York: Pergammon, pp. 291–321.

Daley, D. 1988. *Relapse prevention: Treatment alternatives and counseling aids.* Bradenton, Fla.: Human Services Institute.

Daley, D., H. Moss, and F. Campbell. 1987. *Dual disorders: Counseling clients with chemical dependency and mental illness.* Center City, Minn.: Hazelden.

Daley, D., and M. Raskin, eds. 1990. *Treating the chemically dependent and their families.* Newbury Park, Calif.: Sage.

Ellis, A., J. F. McInerney, R. DiGuiseppe, and R. Yeager. 1988. *Rational-emotive therapy with alcoholics and substance abusers.* Elmsford, New York: Pergammon.

Garner, D. M., and P. E. Garfinkel. 1988. *Diagnostic issues in anorexia nervosa and bulimia nervosa.* New York: Brunner/Mazel.

Johnson, W. G., ed. 1989. *Advances in eating disorders,* vol. 2. Greenwich, Conn.: JAI Press.

Law, R., ed. 1989. *Relapse prevention for sex offenders.* New York: Guilford Press.

Marlatt, G. A. 1985. Lifestyle modification. In G. A. Marlatt and J. R. Gordon, eds. *Relapse Prevention: Maintenance Strategies in the Treatment of Addictive Behaviors.* New York: Guilford Press, 280–350.

Marlatt, G. A., and J. R. Gordon, eds. 1985. *Relapse prevention: Strategies for the Maintenance of behavior change.* New York: Guilford Press.

Meyer, R. E. 1986. How to understand the relationship between psychopathology and addictive disorders. In R. E. Meyer, ed. *Psychopathology and Addictive Disorders.* New York: Guilford Press, 1–16.

Michelson, L., and L. M. Ascher. 1987. *Anxiety and stress disorders.* New York: Guilford Press.

Millon, T. 1981. *Disorders of personality.* New York: John Wiley and Sons.

Nace, E. P. 1987. *The treatment of alcoholism.* New York: Brunner/Mazel.

National Institute of Alcohol Abuse and Alcoholism. 1987. *Alcohol and health: Sixth special report to the U.S. Congress.* Rockville, Md.: NIAAA.

National Institute on Drug Abuse. 1987. *Drug abuse and drug abuse research.* Rockville, Md.: NIDA.

Pattison, E., and E. Kaufman, eds. 1982. *Encyclopedic handbook of alcoholism.* New York: Gardner Press.

Schuckit, M. 1989. *Drug and alcohol abuse: A clinical guide to diagnosis and treatment.* 3d ed. New York: Plenum.

Sternberg, B. 1985. Relapse in weight control: Definitions, processes, and prevention strategies. In G. A. Marlatt and J. R. Gordon, eds. *Relapse Prevention: Maintenance Strategies in the Treatment of Addictive Behaviors.* New York: Guilford Press, 521–45.

Tims, F., and C. Leukefeld, eds. 1987. *Relapse and recovery in drug abuse.* National Institute of Drug Abuse Research Monograph 72. Rockville, Md: NIDA.

Wallace, J. 1985. *Alcoholism: New light on the disease.* Newport, R.I.: Edgehill Publications.

Washton, A. 1989. *Cocaine addiction: Treatment, recovery, and relapse prevention.* New York: Norton.

Zackon, F. 1989. Relapse and "re-joyment": Observations and reflections. In D. Daley, ed. *Relapse: Conceptual research, and clinical perspectives.* New York: Haworth, 67–80.

Zackon, F., W. McAuliffe, and J. Ch'ien. 1985. *Addict aftercare: Recovery training and self-help.* Rockville, Md.: National Institute of Drug Abuse.

Zimberg, S., J. Wallace, and S. Blume, eds. 1985. *Practical approaches to alcoholism psychotherapy,* 2d ed. New York: Plenum Press.

JOURNAL ARTICLES FOR PROFESSIONALS

Bedi, A., and J. Halikas. 1985. Alcoholism and affective disorder. *Alcoholism: Clinical and Experimental Research* 9(2): 133–34.

Behar, D., G. Winokur, and C. Berg. 1984. Depression in the abstinent alcoholic. *American Journal of Psychiatry* 141(9): 1105–7.

Bulik, C. 1987. Drug and alcohol abuse by bulimic women and their families. *American Journal of Psychiatry* 144(12): 1604–6.

Cloninger, C. R. 1987. Neurogenetic adaptive mechanisms in alcoholism. *Science,* 410–17.

Helzer, J., and T. Pryzbeck. 1988. The occurrence of alcoholism with other psychiatric disorders in the general population and its impact on treatment. *Journal of Studies on Alcohol,* 49 (3): 219–24.

Kranzler, H. R., and N. R. Liebowitz. 1988. Anxiety and depression in substance abuse. *Medical Clinics of North America* 72 (4): 867–85.

Lesieur, H. R., S. B. Blume, and R. M. Zoppa. 1986. Alcoholism, drug abuse and gambling. *Alcoholism Clinical and Experimental Research* 10: 33–38.

Marcus, M. D., R. R. Wing, L. Ewing, et al. 1990. Psychiatric-disorders among obese binge eaters. *International Journal of Eating Disorders* 9(1): 69–77.

McCrady, B. 1985. Relative effectiveness of differing components of spouse-involved alcoholism treatment. *Substance Abuse* 6(1): 12–15.

McLellan, A. T., L. Luborsky, and G. E. Woody. 1983. Predicting response to alcohol and drug abuse treatments: Role of psychiatric severity. *Archives of General Psychiatry.* (40): 620–25.

Mirin, S., and R. Weiss. 1988. Psychopathology in substance abusers: Diagnosis and treatment. *American Journal of Drug and Alcohol Abuse* 14(2), 139–58.

Nathan, P. E. 1988. The addictive personality is the behavior of the addict. *Journal of Consulting and Clinical Psychology* 56(2): 183–88.

Simons, A. D., P. J. Lustman, G. E. Murphy, et al. 1985. Predicting response to cognitive therapy of depression: The role of learned resourcefulness. *Cognitive Therapy and Research* 9: 79–89.

Smail, P., T. Stockwell, S. Canter, and R. Hodgson. 1984. Alcohol dependence and phobic anxiety states, I. A prevalence study. *British Journal of Psychiatry* 144: 53–57.

Washton, A. 1986. Nonpharmacologic treatment of cocaine abuse. *Psychiatric Clinics of North America* 9(3): 563–71.

Weiss, K., and D. Rosenberg. 1985. Prevalence of anxiety disorder among alcoholics. *Journal of Clinical Psychiatry* 46(1): 3–5.

Yeary, J. D., and C. L. Heck. 1989. Dual diagnosis: Eating disorders and psychoactive substance dependence. *Journal of Psychoactive Drugs* 21(2): 239–50.

Books, Guides, and Information for Patients and Families

Ackerman, R., and S. Pickering. 1989. *Abused no more: Recovery for women from abusive or co-dependent relationships*. Blue Ridge Summit, Penn.: TAB Books.

Al-Anon. 1981. *Al-Anon's 12 Steps and 12 Traditions*. New York: Al-Anon Family Group.

Alcoholics Anonymous. 1976. *Alcoholics Anonymous (Big Book)*. 3d ed. New York: Alcoholics Anonymous World Services.

————. 1984. *The A.A. member—medications and other drugs*. New York: Alcoholics Anonymous World Services.

Anxiety Disorders. 1988. Washington, D.C.: American Psychiatric Association.

Beattie, M. 1987. *Codependent no more: How to stop controlling others and start caring for yourself*. New York: Harper/Hazelden.

Bill, B. 1981. *Compulsive Overeater*. Minneapolis, Minn.: CompCare.

————. 1986. *Maintenance for compulsive overeaters*. Minneapolis, Minn.: CompCare.

Brownell, K. 1989. *The LEARN program for weight control*. Philadelphia, Penn.: Kelly Brownell.

Burns, D. D. 1980. *Feeling good: The new mood therapy*. New York: William Morrow.

Carnes, P. 1989. *A gentle path through the twelve steps*. Minneapolis, Minn.: Comp Care.

National Council on Alcoholism. *Compulsive gambling: A concern for families with alcoholism and other drug problems*. 1987. New York: NCA.

Custer, R., and H. Milt. 1985. *When luck runs out: Help for compulsive gamblers and their families*. New York: Warner Books.

Daley, D. 1986. *Relapse prevention workbook*. Holmes Beach, Fla.: Learning Publications.

————. 1987. *Family recovery workbook: For families affected by chemical dependency*. Bradenton, Fla.: Human Services Institute.

————. 1988. *Surviving addiction: A guide for alcoholics, drug addicts and their families*. New York: Gardner Press.

————. 1990. *Surviving addiction workbook: Practical tips on developing a recovery plan*. Holmes Beach, Fla.: Learning Publications.

Daley, D., and F. Campbell. 1989. *Coping with dual disorders: chemical dependency and mental illness*. Center City, Minn.: Hazelden.

Damon, J. 1988. *Shopaholics*. Los Angeles, Calif.: Price Stern Sloan.

Ebitt, J. 1987. *The eating illness workbook*. Chicago, Ill.: Parkside.

Gamblers Anonymous. 1984. *Sharing recovery through gamblers anonymous.* Los Angeles, Calif.: Gamblers Anonymous.

———. 1988. *What is GA?* Center City, Minn.: Hazelden.

Gold, M. S. 1989. *The good news about panic, anxiety, and phobias.* New York: Villard Books.

Goodwin, D. 1988. *Is alcoholism hereditary?* New York: Ballantine.

Gowan, W. D. 1988. *Early signs of compulsive gambling.* Center City, Minn.: Hazelden.

Heineman, M. 1988. *When someone you love gambles.* Center City, Minn.: Hazelden.

Hollis, J. 1985. *Fat is a family affair.* Center City, Minn.: Hazelden.

Hope and recovery: A twelve step guide for healing from compulsive sexual behavior. 1987. Minneapolis, Minn.: CompCare.

Lesieur, H. R. 1986. *Understanding compulsive gambling.* Center City, Minn.: Hazelden Educational Services.

Lewinsohn, P. M., et al. 1986. *Control your depression.* New York: Prentice-Hall Press.

Mundis, J. 1988. *How to get out of debt, stay out of debt and live prosperously.* New York: Bantam.

Overeaters Anonymous. 1980. Torrance, Calif.: Overeaters Anonymous.

Papolos, D. F., and J. Papolos. 1987. *Overcoming Depression.* New York: Harper & Row.

Rosellini, G., and M. Worden. 1988. *Here comes the sun.* Center City, Minn.: Hazelden

———. 1990. *Of course you're anxious.* Center City, Minn.: Hazelden.

Schaeffer, B. 1987. *Is it love or is it addiction?* Center City, Minn.: Hazelden.

Sex and love addicts anonymous. 1986. Boston, Mass.: The Augustine Fellowship.

Sheehan, D. V. 1984. *The anxiety disease.* New York: Charles Scribner & Sons.

Siegel, M., J. Brisman, and M. Weinshel. 1988. *Surviving an eating disorder: Strategies for family and friends.* New York: Harper & Row.

Wilson, R. R. 1989. *Breaking the panic cycle: Self-help for people with phobias.* Rockville, Md.: Phobia Society of America.

Worden, M. 1990. *Depression and recovery from chemical dependency.* Center City, Minn.: Hazelden.

Self-Help Organizations

Following is a list of national clearinghouses of self-help organizations. Many people recovering from an addictive disorder find it helpful to participate in self-help programs. Many of these self-help organizations have local branches. You may wish to consult your telephone directory or ask a professional in a mental health or chemical-dependency treatment program about the availability of local services.

American Anorexia/Bulimia Association, Inc. (AABA). 133 Cedar Lane, Teaneck, NJ 07666.

Anorexia Nervosa and Related Eating Disorders, Inc. P. O. Box 5102, Eugene, OR 97405.

Anorexics/Bulimics Anonymous (ABA). P. O. Box 112214, San Diego, CA 92111.

Cocaine Anonymous. 6125 Washington Boulevard, Suite 202, Los Angeles, CA 90230.

Co-Dependents Anonymous. P. O. Box 33577, Phoenix, AZ 85067-3577.

Gam-Anon International Service Office. P. O. Box 157, Whitestone, New York, NY 11357.

Gamblers Anonymous, International Service Office. P. O. Box 17173, Los Angeles, CA 90017.

Marijuana Addicts Anonymous. P. O. Box 8354, Berkeley, CA 94704.

Marijuana Anonymous. P. O. Box 2912, Van Nuys, CA 91404.

Nar-Anon Family Groups. P. O. Box 2562, Palos Verdes, CA 90274.

National Depressive and Manic Depressive Association. Merchandise Mart, P. O. Box 3395, Chicago, IL 60654.

Overeaters Anonymous World Service Office. P. O. Box 92870, Torrance, CA 90009

Prostitutes Anonymous. P. O. Box 2620, Ventnor, NJ 08406.

Sex & Love Addicts Anonymous (SLAA). Augustine Fellowship, P. O. Box 119, New Town Branch, Boston, MA 02258.

Sex Addicts Anonymous (SAA). P. O. Box 3038, Minneapolis, MN 55403.

Sexaholics Anonymous (SA). P. O. Box 300, Simi Valley, CA 93062.

ToughLove. P. O. Box 1069, Doylestown, PA 18901.

Women for Sobriety. P. O. Box 618, Quakertown, PA 18951.

About the Author

Dennis C. Daley, M.S.W., has worked for many years with individuals experiencing addictions and other mental health problems. Mr. Daley holds faculty positions at several universities and lectures throughout the country on addiction and recovery. He is currently an assistant professor of psychiatry and director of the Office of Family Studies and Social Work at the University of Pittsburgh School of Medicine, affiliated with the Western Psychiatric Institute and Clinic. He has written many articles, over twenty books and recovery guides, and four educational films on addiction and recovery, family recovery, relapse prevention, and dual disorders (addiction combined with mental illness). His educational films and practical recovery materials are used in many treatment programs throughout the United States and in other countries.

Other Books, Recovery Guides, and Articles by Dennis C. Daley

A Parent's Guide to Alcoholism and Drug Abuse
Practical Advice on Recovery and Relapse Prevention

Coping with Dual Disorders
Clinical Dependency and Mental Illness

Dual Disorders
Clinical Dependency and Mental Illness

Family Recovery Workbook
For Families Affected by Chemical Dependency

I Can Talk about What Hurts
A Book for Kids in Homes Where There's Chemical Dependency

Relapse
A Guide to Successful Recovery

Relapse
Conceptual, Research, and Clinical Perspectives

Relapse Prevention
Treatment Alternatives and Counseling Aids

Relapse Prevention Workbook
For Recovering Alcoholics and Drug Dependent Persons

Surviving Addiction
A Guide for Alcoholics, Drug Addicts, and Their Families

Taking Care of Yourself
When a Family Member has Dual Disorders

Adolescent Relapse Prevention Workbook

Changing Personality Traits
A Guide to Self-Improvement

Chemical Dependency and Mental Illness
A Resource Guide on Dual Disorders

Counselor Wellness
Avoiding Burnout and Managing Stress

Double Trouble
Chemical Dependency and Mental Illness

Getting High and Doing Time
What's the Connection?

Staying Sober, Keeping Straight

Surviving Addiction Workbook

Together
Families in Recovery

Treating the Chemically Dependent and Their Families

Working through Denial
The Key to Recovery